British Railways
The First 25 Years

Volume 8
North East England

County Durham and North Yorkshire
(between York and Newcastle)

'B16/2' 4-6-0 No. 61437 approaching Seamer station from Scarborough in around 1954 with an interesting train of mainly L&NER and BR stock but with a Great Central Railway matchboard coach near the rear. The 'B16/2' was a Gresley rebuild introduced in 1937 of the Raven NER 1920 design replacing the Stephenson valve gear by Walschaerts with derived motion for the inside cylinder.

BRITISH RAILWAYS

The First 25 Years

Volume 8 – North East England
County Durham and North Yorkshire
(between York and Newcastle)

J. Allan and A. Murray

Lightmoor Press

Dieselisation came to the area from 1957 when large numbers of diesel multiple units were delivered, and this continued through to the end of 1959. The most common type was this Metropolitan-Cammell design, later Class '101', which configured in two-, three- or four-car sets according to the services they were used on. South Gosforth-allocated Driving Trailer Composite No. E56079 with South Shields on the destination blind stands at Durham on 28th August 1963.

Cover photographs

Front upper:
'Deltic' No. D9006 near Darlington with the southbound 'Flying Scotsman' in 1964. No. D9006 was unnamed until December of that year when it was christened The Fife and Forfar Yeomanry. Note the two Mark II Corridor Firsts introduced into the 'Scotsman' set in 1964.

Front lower:
'A8' 4-6-2T No. 69854 at Darlington Bank Top with a train to Saltburn and Middlesbrough on 14th April 1956. Until displaced by DMUs in 1957 these big passenger tanks were used on the extensive service on this route, which in 1955 had no less than thirty-six departures each day from Darlington.

Back upper:
'J27' 0-6-0 No. 65885 at Ryhope in September 1966. It was one of the last of the class to be built, emerging from Darlington Works in June 1923.

Back centre:
'Austerity' 2-8-0 No. 90048 on the turntable in the round-house at Thornaby on 25th September 1960. It had been transferred there in August 1959 from West Hartlepool.

Back lower:
English Electric Type '3' No. D6768 near Sedgefield, heading for Stockton from the Ferry Hill direction, on 6th May 1964. No. D6768 was the last one of the 1962 batch built by English Electric at Vulcan Foundry. It went straight to Thornaby where it remained until October 1971. It was renumbered under TOPS as No. 37068 in January 1974 and then No. 37356 in June 1988 after it was re-geared with CP7 bogies.

© Lightmoor Press, J. Allan, A. Murray, 2019.
Designed by Stephen Phillips.

British Library Cataloguing-in-Publication Data.
A catalogue record for this book is available from the British Library.
ISBN 978-1-911038-60-3

All rights reserved. No part of this publication may be reproduced, stored in a retrieval system or transmitted in any form or by any means, electronic, mechanical, photocopying, recording or otherwise, without the written permission of the publisher.

LIGHTMOOR PRESS
Unit 144B, Lydney Trading Estate, Harbour Road, Lydney, Gloucestershire GL15 4EJ
www.lightmoor.co.uk

Lightmoor Press is an imprint of
Black Dwarf Lightmoor Publications Ltd.

Printed in Poland
www.lfbookservices.co.uk

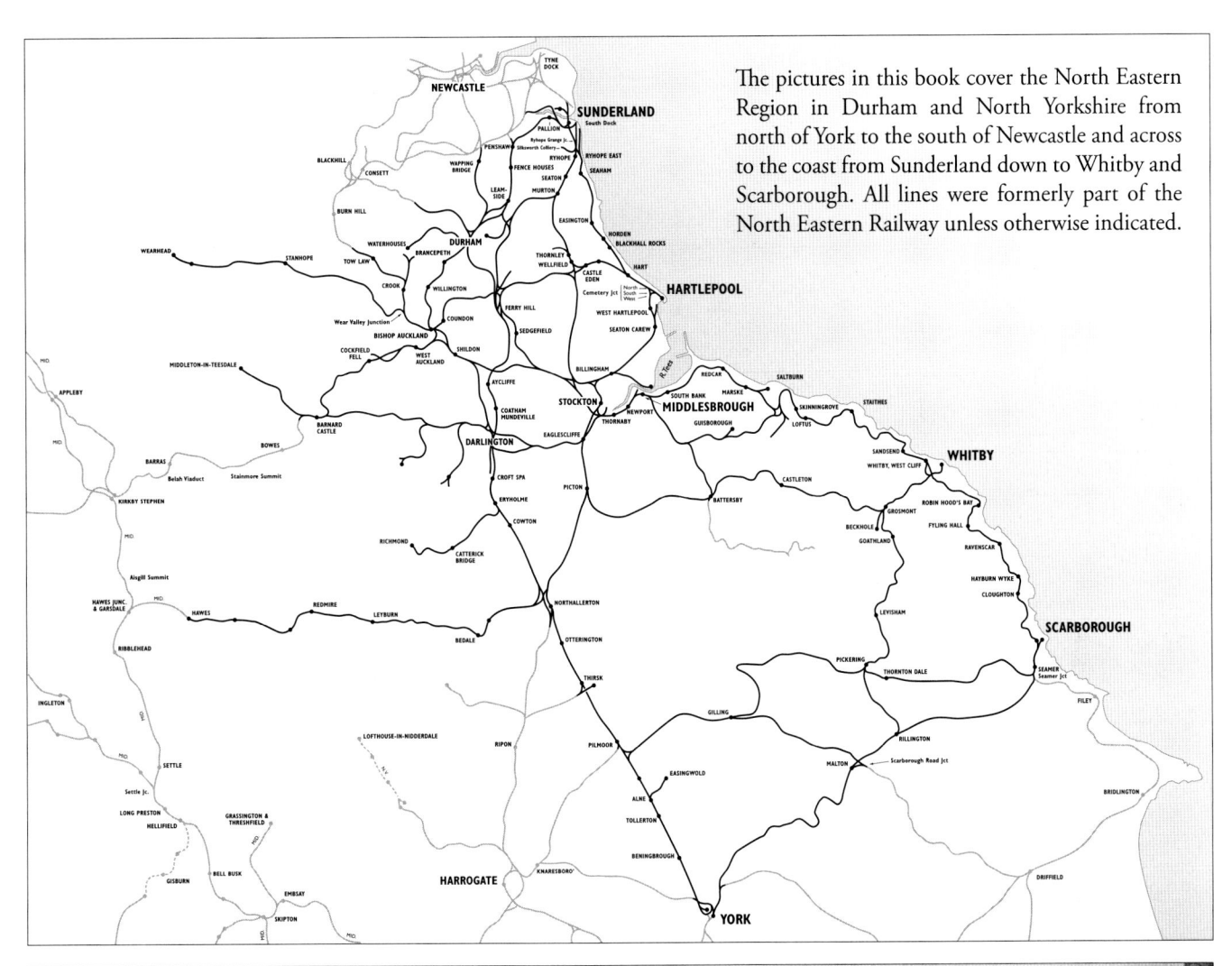

The pictures in this book cover the North Eastern Region in Durham and North Yorkshire from north of York to the south of Newcastle and across to the coast from Sunderland down to Whitby and Scarborough. All lines were formerly part of the North Eastern Railway unless otherwise indicated.

The 'Q6' 0-8-0s along with the 'J27' 0-6-0s were the mainstay of the freight traffic up until the end of North Eastern Region steam in 1967. The now-preserved No. 63395 is about to pass Seaham signal box with northbound loaded hopper wagons in 1966.

Contents

Introduction and Acknowledgements	7

1	**East Coast main line between York and Darlington**	**8**
	Beningbrough	8
	Tollerton	9
	Alne	10
	Pilmoor	11
	Thirsk	15
	Otterington	20
	Northallerton	21
	Cowton	26
	Eryholme	27
	Croft Spa	28

2	**Darlington**	**29**
	Bank Top	29
	North Road station	43
	Works	45
	Shed	52
	Haughton Road	60

3	**Northwards from Darlington**	**61**
	East Coast main line to Durham	61
	Darlington-Durham via Shildon and Bishop Auckland	67
	Durham	71
	Durham to Sunderland	78

4	**North Yorkshire and Durham branches and secondary lines**	**82**
	The Easingwold Railway	82
	The Wensleydale Branch – Northallerton to Hawes	84
	Richmond	87
	Bishop Auckland to Crook and Tow Law	88
	Bishop Auckland to Barnard Castle	94
	Middleton-in-Teesdale	100
	The Wearhead Branch	103

5	**Sunderland to Hartlepool**	**104**
	South from Sunderland	107
	Sunderland South Dock shed	111
	Ryhope Grange Junction	114
	Ryhope Colliery Junction and the Silksworth Colliery Branch	116
	The Durham and Sunderland Railway	120
	The inland route between Sunderland and Hartlepool	121
	Along the coast to Hartlepool	123
	West Hartlepool	133

6	**Teesside**	**146**
	Seaton Carew	146
	Billingham	146
	Middlesbrough	148
	Thornaby	152
	Thornaby Depot	153
	Newport	159
	South Bank	160
	Stockton	160
	Eaglescliffe	163
	Sedgefield	164

7	**Malton to Pickering and the North Yorkshire Moors**	**165**
	Malton	165
	Pickering	169
	The North Yorkshire Moors line	171

8	**To the seaside – Whitby and Scarborough**	**175**
	Middlesbrough to Whitby along the coast	175
	The Esk Valley line	181
	Guisborough	182
	Whitby	183
	Whitby to Scarborough	188
	Seamer	191
	Scarborough	194

'B1' 4-6-0 No. 61021 *Reitbok* waits for departure time in Platform 2 at Whitby Town in 1964. On the right is a Metropolitan-Cammell DMU, the most numerous type used on the North Eastern Region.

Introduction and Acknowledgements

This is the eighth in a series of books, depicting the first 25 years of British Railways, which will eventually cover the whole of the UK. We have been fortunate to have had access to hundreds of different pictures from which to choose the final selection presented here. At an early stage, we made the decision to include photographs spanning the early British Railways era through to the pre-TOPS diesels, although the emphasis is on that interesting transitional period of the late 1950s and early 1960s.

Here we cover the North Eastern Region in North Yorkshire and County Durham between York in the south and Newcastle in the north – both of these important railway cities will be covered in later volumes. We start on the East Coast main line north of York and travel up to Darlington, pausing there to visit the Works and shed, before continuing to Durham but stopping short of Newcastle. After examining some of the branch lines and secondary routes off the main line, we move from these rural areas into the coal and steel producing region, working down from Sunderland to Hartlepool and then on to the heavily industrialised area of Teesside, looking at the new depot built at Thornaby as well as the older steam sheds which provided the locomotives which worked the extensive freight traffic.

We then turn towards the seaside, starting with the line which forms the bottom edge of our route, between York and the east coast via Malton and what is now the North Yorkshire Moors Railway. To complete our journey, we travel down to the North Yorkshire coast from Teeside to Whitby and end at Scarborough, the biggest of several seaside resorts which developed with the railway.

Until 1957 the scene had hardly changed from pre-war days and even pre-grouping in many parts of the area. Freight traffic remained in the hands of the NER 'J27' 0-6-0s and 'Q6' 0-8-0s while local passenger work was dominated by 'G5' 0-4-4Ts and the big 4-6-2Ts on the heavier services. British Railways Standard designs had a limited impact on some of the secondary work in the mid-1950s but the Gresley engines continued to rule on the East Coast main line until the end of the decade. The first sign of sweeping changes arose when large numbers of diesel multiple units arrived from 1957 onwards, sweeping away the passenger tanks within a couple of years.

Dieselisation of the main line passenger services started in around 1960 with the English Electric Type '4' but 1961 was to see the introduction of the 'Deltics', worthy successors to the Gresley Pacifics which were completely displaced by 1964 as the 'Peaks' and Brush Type '4's took over the rest of their work. However, steam continued on some of the heavy freight work until 1967 although BR Sulzer Type '2's and English Electric Type '3's began to take over from around 1962. The North Eastern Region merged into the Eastern Region on 1st January 1967 but, for simplicity, we refer to the North Eastern Region throughout this book.

Acknowledgements

Our thanks again go to Vic Smith, Steve Phillips and also to John Atkinson for their help. Any errors remaining are of course entirely the responsibility of the authors and publishers.

Almost all of the photographs in this volume are from *www.Rail-Online.co.uk* including those from Rail Archive Stephenson, together with a handful from the Ben Brooksbank collection. We have taken the opportunity to include many full page portraits which pay tribute to the quality of some of these early photographs.

References

We have consulted a number of sources to provide details of locomotives and workings. In particular, the RCTS BR Standard series, *Yeadon's Register of LNER Locomotives*, the Irwell Press 'Book of' series, the Roger Harris series *The Allocation History of BR Diesels and Electrics* and also several websites, *www.railcar.co.uk*, *www.napier-chronicles.co.uk*, *www.derbysulzers.com* and *www.class47.co.uk*.

J. Allan and A. Murray 2019

1 – East Coast main line between York and Darlington

The line from York to Darlington was opened in 1841 by the Great North of England Railway which, after several amalgamations, came into the ownership of the North Eastern Railway in 1854. New colour light signalling was installed in the 1930s on what enthusiasts termed the 'Racing Stretch' between York and Northallerton and most of the line was widened to cope with the pressures of freight traffic, although the final section between Alne and Pilmoor was not completed until 1960.

Beningbrough

WD 'Austerity' 2-8-0 No. 90081 at Beningbrough in the mid-1950s with a northbound Class 'F' express freight made up of all unfitted stock. It was allocated to Newport, one of the sheds replaced by Thornaby when it was modernised in 1958. As with other 'Austerities', No. 90081 had several numbers, starting with No. 77290 when it was built in 1944, No. 3081 in 1947, No. 63081 in 1948 and finally No. 90081 in November 1950. Beningbrough station was closed to passengers in 1958 and lost its remaining freight services in 1965.

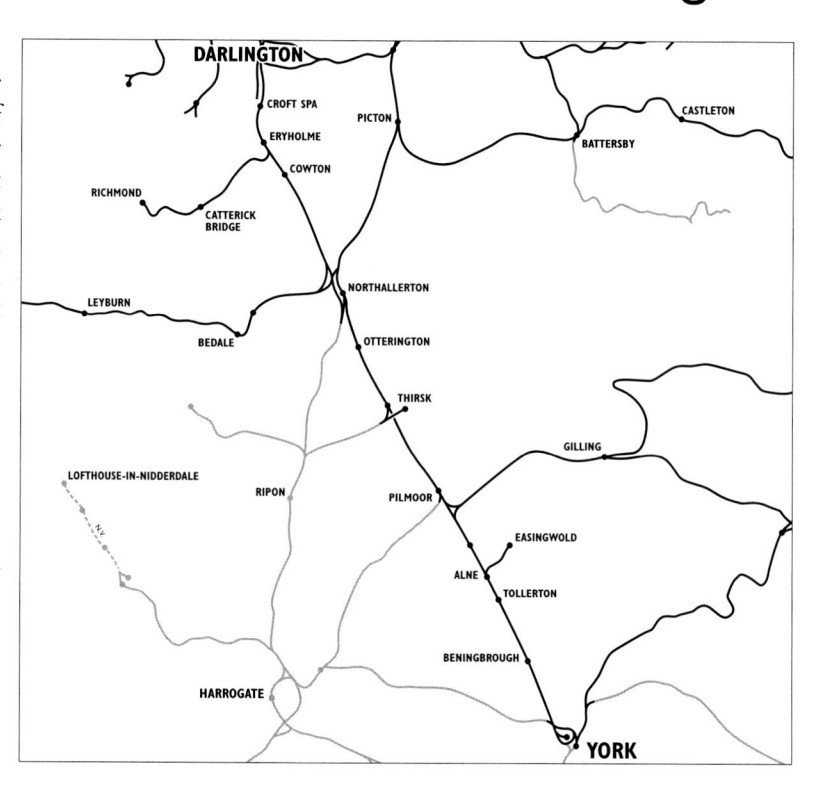

Tollerton

'Deltic' No. D9001 *St. Paddy* passes Tollerton signal box with the 11am King's Cross - Glasgow Queen Street in 1962. It was the first of the twenty-two production series 'Deltics' to emerge from Vulcan Foundry, arriving at Doncaster on 16th January 1961, but did not go into traffic until 23rd February. This was five days before No. D9000 which had been held back at the English Electric works because it was being fitted with an experimental flashing warning light. No. D9001 was named *St. Paddy* on 7th July 1961 at Doncaster Works, without ceremony, in honour of a racehorse which won the 1960 Derby. Note the 1A22 headcode, the 'A' signifying a train running on the East Coast main line between London, Newcastle and Scotland irrespective of whether it was an Up or Down working. The striking modern signal box was opened in January 1961 as part of the signalling upgrade of the East Coast main line after the completion of the quadrupling projects in 1960. The walls were inclined at 8½ degrees to reduce glare and reflection from the windows and the flat roof had a large overhang. Tollington box closed in 1989 when a new facility at York took over.

Cecil Ord/RailArchive Stephenson

Alne

English Electric Type '3' No. D6769 with a southbound Class '7' freight at Alne in July 1966. It was at Thornaby from new in July 1962 and stayed there until 1992, and as TOPS No. 37069 was named *Thornaby TMD* in 1986.

English Electric Type '4' No. D240 with a southbound freight approaches the bridge shown in the picture above in July 1966. The Easingwold Railway branched off to the right (see Chapter 4). Brush Type '4's had replaced the class on most East Coast main line Class '1' passenger duties by this date. No. D240 was allocated to Gateshead from new in October 1959 and stayed on the North Eastern Region until it was withdrawn as No. 40040 in 1980.

Pilmoor

Formerly the junction of the The Pilmoor, Boroughbridge and Knaresborough Railway which closed for passengers in 1950 and for goods in 1964, Pilmoor station closed in May 1958. It had platforms on the main line, the two-sided Down side one was also the branch platform.

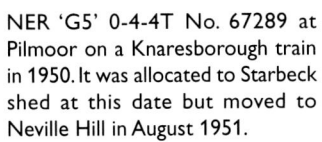

NER 'G5' 0-4-4T No. 67289 at Pilmoor on a Knaresborough train in 1950. It was allocated to Starbeck shed at this date but moved to Neville Hill in August 1951.
Lens of Sutton Association

'D49/1' 4-4-0 No. 62702 *Oxfordshire* passing Pilmoor South signal box in the 1950s. Allocated to York from early 1952, it was fitted with a L&NER 'Group Standard' 4,200 gallon tender and was an early withdrawal, in November 1958. No. 62702 was working a stores train consisting of an ancient ex-NER 6-wheeler and a Gresley Brake Third.

An eight-car train formed of four 'Derby Lightweight' two-car units heads south at Pilmoor under Jobbing Cross bridge in October 1964. These had been built in 1954 and each set had a pair of BUT (AEC) 150hp engines, the same type as used in the pre-war Great Western Railway railcars! Up to four sets could be coupled together but they were incompatible with most of the later DMUs and had a Yellow Diamond coupling code; this ensured their early withdrawal by 1969.

Freight work was the staple diet for the English Electric Type '4's in the late 1960s. Photographed from the bridge in the picture above D253 is working a northbound train at Pilmoor in May 1967. Allocated to York since it entered traffic in January 1960, D253 moved to Gateshead in 1975. It was withdrawn as TOPS No. 40253 in 1976 after a collision in Scotland. The Up Slow line with concrete sleepers (on the left of the picture) over the five miles between Pilmoor and Alne was only completed in 1960; prior to that around 130 southbound trains per day, ranging from slow, heavy freights to the named East Coast expresses, had to use the single Up line.

No. D1100 with the Cliffe-Uddingston cement train at Pilmoor in May 1967. The make-up of the train is interesting train with a Southern Railway brake van followed by eleven Standard Railway Wagon Company built APCM vans carrying bagged cement and then cement tanks with another brake van at the rear. Although No. D1100 was the lowest numbered Brush Type '4', it was actually one of the last to be built, entering traffic in August 1966, and allocated to York. It was transferred to Gateshead in March 1967 and became No. 47298 under TOPS.

No. D9010 *The King's Own Scottish Borderer* was the only 'Deltic' to have BR double arrow symbols while still in original two-tone green livery. These were applied in December 1966 along with the full yellow ends. No. D9010 was working the 11.00 Newcastle-King's Cross when photographed at Pilmoor in October 1967.

Ten of the final batch of English Electric Type '1' Bo-Bos, by then Class '20', which entered service in early 1967 went to York. They had Corporate blue livery with full yellow ends and four-character headcode boxes from new as shown by No. D8307 and a classmate at Pilmoor in March 1968. All ten were transferred to Tinsley in October 1971. No. D8307 became No. 20207 under TOPS and was withdrawn in 1983 after a collision when working on the Scottish Region.

Class '37' No. D6778 heads north with an unfitted freight at Pilmoor in June 1968. Diesel brake tenders were common on such freight workings in this area in the late 1960s; in their later years propelling was banned. No. D6778 is still in green but has full yellow ends; it was allocated to Thornaby from new in October 1962 until October 1971 when it moved to March. It was renumbered as No. 37078 under TOPS and was named *Teesside Steelmaster* in 1984.

Thirsk

'A1' No. 60142 *Edward Fletcher* from Heaton approaching Thirsk station with a northbound parcels train on 23rd August 1962. It would shortly move further north to Tweedmouth, officially on the 9th September, but would return to Tyneside in October 1964 for its last eight months of service.

Darlington-allocated 'B1' 4-6-0 No. 61382 runs through Thirsk with a northbound Class 'F' train of empty mineral wagons on 23rd August 1962. It would move to the Leeds area in June of the following year, firstly to Copley Hill then Ardsley, ending its career there on 7th December 1964.

'B1' 4-6-0 No. 61382 continues north on 23rd August 1962. In the distance is Thirsk signal box, commissioned in 1933 as part of the York to Darlington re-signalling using three-aspect colour light signals, controlled by mainly new manual signal boxes. Thirsk was the exception because it was a new box which had a route setting panel of 'thumb switches'.

The serviceman sitting on Platform 3 does not look up from his newspaper as York-allocated English Electric Type '4' No. D259 thunders through Thirsk on 23rd August 1962.

Deltic No. D9015 *Tulyar* rushes through Thirsk on 23rd August 1962 with the Up 'Flying Scotsman', still immaculate after a recent works visit when it gained its yellow warning panel. The timetable from 18th June to 9th September 1962 was the first with diagrams for the full 'Deltic' fleet of twenty-two locomotives. After it was taken out of service in January 1982 *Tulyar* was put up for auction at Christie's auction house in December 1982 along with five nameplates from the class. However, the highest bid of £5,500 fell well short of the £10,000 reserve price – although the nameplates were all snapped up! Fortunately, it was purchased privately in 1984 and then by the Deltic Preservation Society in 1986 and is currently (2019) being restored at Barrow Hill.

On the same day, No. D9018 *Ballymoss* runs through Thirsk heading the Down 'Elizabethan' from King's Cross to Edinburgh complete with a steam-style headboard. It is still in its as-delivered condition without the small yellow warning panel which it gained at the end of the year.

The final shot from our busy cameraman at Thirsk on Thursday 23rd August 1962 is of 'Deltic' No. D9017 *The Durham Light Infantry* working the Down 'Flying Scotsman'. The 'Deltics' looked dull from the front before the green was relieved by the yellow warning panels. No. D9017 entered service in November 1961 and received its warning panels in March 1963 and full yellow ends in April 1967, before repainting in Rail Blue in October 1969. It was allocated to Gateshead from new until May 1979, transferring to York for its last two years before withdrawal.

Class '45' No. D127 with a Newcastle to Liverpool express, probably in 1969 before it was repainted in blue during November. Thirsk was a bleak looking station despite retaining its L&NER lighting. No. D127 was renumbered as No. 45072 in 1974 and was in service until 1985.

Class '37' No. D6773, which appears to have recently been repainted in Corporate blue livery, with an Up freight south of Thirsk station. It has just passed under the bridge formerly carrying the ex-Leeds Northern Railway line to Thirsk Town, which closed as a goods-only station on 3rd October 1966. Note the loading of square-baled hay direct onto a flat-bed lorry for onward sale. This would indicate that the date is August or early September, probably in 1970.

Class '46' No. D181 in a photograph taken in the same place, also with a southbound Class '7' freight. It had been repainted into blue livery in 1967 as can be judged by its condition compared to No. D6773 above, although the fact that it was a Gateshead locomotive may have contributed to its condition. No. D181 became No. 46044 under TOPS and continued to work until 1984.

Otterington

English Electric Type '4' No. D281 with an Up express in February 1966 approaching Otterington station, between Northallerton and Thirsk, and was photographed from the Station Road bridge. It was delivered to York from Newton-le-Willows in June 1960 and was there until March 1967 when it was transferred to Gateshead. Renumbered to No. 40081 in 1974, it worked until early 1983.

Northallerton

Northallerton, thirty miles north of York and fourteen miles south of Darlington was where the Leeds Northern Railway from Ripon to Stockton and Teesside passed beneath the East Coast main line. North of the station was the triangular junction for the Wensleydale Branch to Hawes and Garsdale.

The Stephenson Locomotive Society and Manchester Locomotive Society ran the 'Northern Dales Rail Tour' from Manchester Victoria on 4th September 1955. LM&SR Compound No. 41102 took the first leg to Tebay handing over to 'J21' No. 65061 and Ivatt Class '2' No. 46478 for a journey over the Stainmore line to Darlington North Road. NER 'A8' 4-6-2T No. 69855 carried on to Northallerton via Eaglescliffe and Yarm. From Northallerton it was joined by 'D20' 4-4-0 No. 62360 to Hawes and Garsdale where No. 41102 returned the party to Manchester.

In the upper picture No. 62360 has just backed onto the train while No. 69855 waits alongside. In the lower picture, in a scene which would give a heart attack to a modern-day Health & Safety officer, the pair are ready to depart once the pictures have been taken and the tracks cleared.

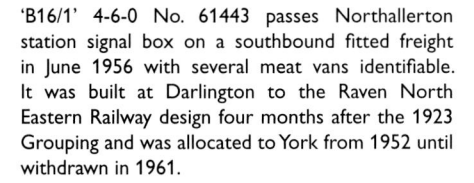

'B16/1' 4-6-0 No. 61443 passes Northallerton station signal box on a southbound fitted freight in June 1956 with several meat vans identifiable. It was built at Darlington to the Raven North Eastern Railway design four months after the 1923 Grouping and was allocated to York from 1952 until withdrawn in 1961.

York 'A2' Pacific No. 60526 *Sugar Palm* comes off the Stockton line with a southbound express. After 1954 all expresses from Stockton or originating from the Hartlepool line were routed via Darlington rather than the direct route. The East Coast main line to Darlington continues in a straight line to the left of the picture and on the right is the coal depot. The siding immediately behind the signal box led to a turntable.

NER 'G5' 0-4-4T No. 67324 at Northallerton on a Wensleydale train in the early 1950s. The class worked the branch passenger trains from the end of 1929 onwards, although 'D20' 4-4-0s took over some of the trains after nationalisation.

An 'A3' relegated to freight work in the mid-1960s heads a Down fitted train with two L&NER 12-ton plywood goods vans (Diag. 195) and a 'Conflat' at the front. The Pacific has 'German' style smoke deflectors but a Great Northern Railway pattern coal-railed tender. The train for the Ripon line is waiting in the bay platform under the canopy on the right of the picture; this service was withdrawn in March 1967. The electric lights on the platforms were installed in 1957.

A '9F' 2-10-0 from New England, No. 92034 passes through Northallerton with a northbound freight in the early 1960s. It had been transferred to the Peterborough shed from Frodingham in April 1959 and left for Immingham in June 1963. Parcels vans are stored in the bay under the canopy, Platform 4, formerly used for the Wensleydale line whose passenger services ceased in April 1954. The sign on the left reads 'The Northallerton Live Stock Mart Co. Ltd.'

'A3' 4-6-2 No. 60048 *Doncaster* with a southbound parcels train on 8th April 1961. The train is passing the three-storey high Northallerton station signal box which was commissioned in 1939 as part of an L&NER modernisation scheme which included colour-light re-signalling. The box remained in use until 1990 when the new control centre at York took over. No. 60048 has small chimneyside wing plate smoke deflectors fitted in November 1959, six months after it received a double chimney.

Darlington-allocated NER 'D20' 4-4-0 No. 62388 is being serviced at Northallerton on 3rd June 1950. The shed was accessed off the low-level line from Leeds via Harrogate and the wooden wall of the station forms the background to this picture. The 'D20's were regular engines on the Wensleydale line to Hawes at this time.

The two-road engine shed at Northallerton was situated between the low-level Leeds Northern line and the East Coast main line. The latter was at a higher level as is apparent from this picture looking to the right of the water tower. The shed dated from 1881, having been extended in 1886, but there was no turntable because a 42ft one was provided at the north end of the station along with coaling facilities; it was closed in March 1963. Peppercorn 'K1' 2-6-0 No. 62043 from Darlington is parked partly inside the shed on 19th July 1959.

CHAPTER 1 - EAST COAST MAINLINE BETWEEN YORK AND DARLINGTON

Five BR Standard Class '2' 2-6-0s built at Darlington in 1954, Nos. 78010-78014, were transferred from West Auckland to Northallerton in March 1955 to replace the NER 'J21' and 'J25' 0-6-0s and the 'G5' 0-4-4Ts. They were used on local pick-up freights to Newport, Cowton and Melmerby and also a daily pick-up to York and the Northallerton Low Yard pilot turn. Two of the five, which had been joined by No. 78015 in December 1956, Nos. 78011 and 78014, stand outside the shed, probably in 1963, as they were about to be transferred to Darlington when Northallerton shed closed, hence the absence of shedplates on both engines. Note the Smith-Stone speed indicator working off the rear driving wheel of No. 78011.

Cowton

Peppercorn 'A1' No. 60138 *Boswell* with an Up Class 'E' freight on 2nd May 1964 at Cowton, about seven miles north of Northallerton. No. 60148 was allocated to York from new in December 1948 until it was withdrawn in October 1965.

On the same day, Gresley 'V2' 2-6-2 No. 60808 also heads an Up freight, a Class 'F' comprised of bogie bolsters carrying steel products. No. 60808 was built in 1937 as No. 4779, was renumbered to No. 808 under the 1946 L&NER renumbering scheme and gained its BR number in June 1948; it was allocated to Darlington at the date of this photograph and would be withdrawn within three months. Note the Cowton passing loops either side of the main lines; the Down one is occupied.

No. D291 passes the end of the Cowton goods loops with a northbound express on 23rd August 1962, a duty from which the English Electric Type '4s' would soon be ousted by 'Deltics' and Brush Type '4s'. No. D291 was allocated to Longsight at this date and remained on the London Midland Region until it was withdrawn as No. 40091 in 1983.

Eryholme

The 'Deltic' now preserved in the National Collection, No. D9002 *The King's Own Yorkshire Light Infantry*, speeds through Eryholme on 9th May 1964 with the 'Heart of Midlothian', the 1.30pm from Edinburgh to King's Cross. The branch line from Richmond joined the main line beyond the signal box. Eryholme station was known as Dalton until 1901.

Croft Spa

Twelve two-car diesel unit sets were built by Metropolitan-Cammell in 1957 for the North Eastern Region and allocated to Darlington where they were used on Richmond, Crook and Middleton-in-Teesdale branch trains and on Durham-Bishop Auckland services. On 23rd August 1962, a set working from Richmond to Darlington was crossing the A167 Northallerton Road bridge at Croft-on-Tees, forty-one miles north of York and only a short distance from Darlington.

BR Sulzer 'Peak' No. D63 before it was named *Royal Inniskilling Fusilier* in September 1965 passes through Croft Spa station, which served Croft-on-Tees and Hurworth-on-Tees until 3rd March 1969, with a northbound express. It was built in March 1962, renumbered as No. 45044 in 1975 and withdrawn in 1987. Local services between Darlington and Northallerton stopped using the station in 1958 and it was then only served by trains working down to Eryholme and the Richmond Branch up until closure in March 1969. Presumably the lady on the platform was waiting for one of these to travel into Darlington.

2 – Darlington

The importance of Darlington as a railway centre dates back to the 1820s and the opening of the Stockton & Darlington Railway. From that point onwards Darlington was destined to be a 'Railway Town' and the first station on the S&D was at North Road. In 1841 the Great North of England Railway main line between York and Newcastle was opened. The S&D established its new workshops in the town in 1854 and these developed into the important locomotive works of the NER and L&NER. Darlington Bank Top station was opened in July 1887. However, to many of us it will always be for freight and heavy engineering that Darlington will be remembered. The marshalling yards were extensive and the support industries for the railway comprehensive.

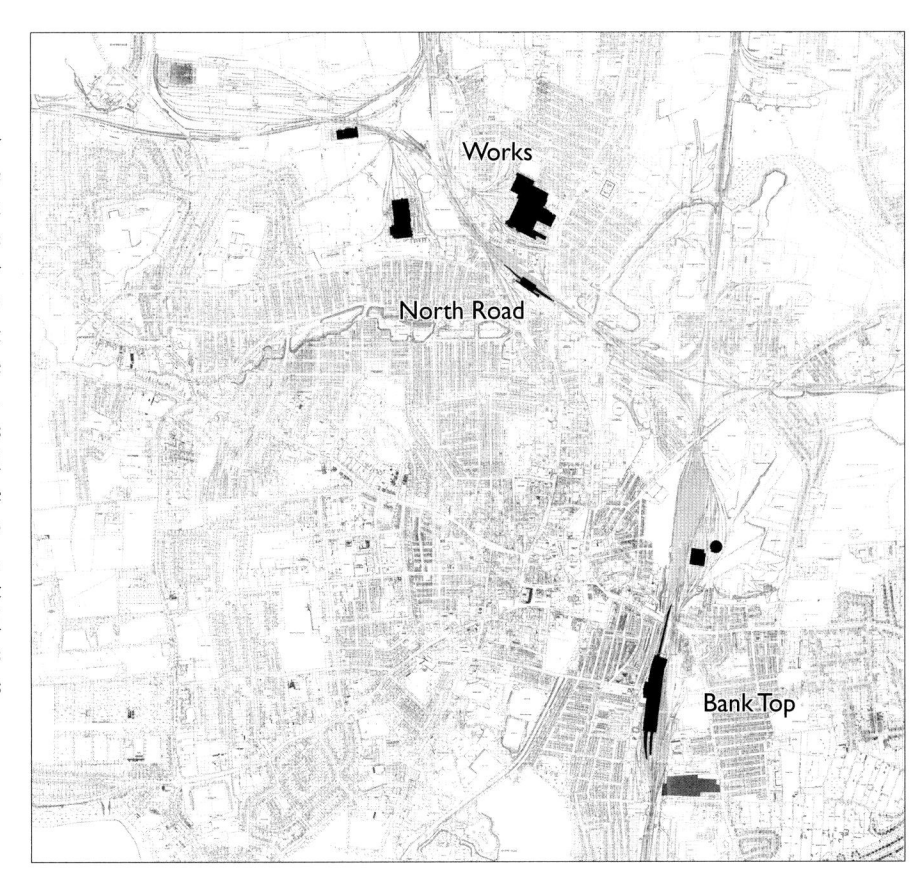

Bank Top

'A4' No. 60027 *Merlin* passing the North signal box at Darlington with the non-stop Up 'Elizabethan', probably in 1956. The 'Elizabethan' ran in the summer months only, and the train was originally called the 'Capitals Limited', changing with the Queen's Coronation in 1953. No. 60027 went through Doncaster Works in June 1956 and these non-stop duties were worked as far as was possible by Haymarket engines freshly outshopped from Works with low, post-overhaul mileages. Note on the right, the children on the shed roofs in front of the prefabricated bungalows which were such a feature of post-war Britain.

'A3' No. 60070 *Gladiateur* waits at Darlington Bank Top on 8th April 1953 with a southbound express. It is surprisingly clean for a Gateshead engine; No. 60070 moved back and forth between there and Darlington seven times between 1948 and 1959 before leaving for the Leeds area.

BR Standard Class '2' 2-6-0 No. 78016 on a freight working at Darlington passes the Cleveland Bridge & Engineering Co. Ltd factory just to the south of the station on 11th April 1954. Built at Darlington in March of that year, it went initially to West Auckland before quickly moving on to Kirkby Stephen along with classmates Nos. 78017 and 78018. They were used on the mineral traffic over Stainmore summit and Darlington-Penrith passenger trains.

CHAPTER 2 - DARLINGTON

'A2/2' No. 60501 *Cock o' the North* gets underway from Darlington with an express to Bristol on 13th April 1957. It was one of six engines rebuilt into Pacifics from Gresley 'P2' 2-8-2s in 1943 and 1944. The rebuilds were ungainly, with the bogie a long way forward of the front coupled wheels, and they suffered from numerous minor faults requiring about three times the number of works repairs needed by the Gresley Pacifics. All six were originally returned to Scotland where the 2-8-2s had been used, but they all were sent south of the Border in late 1949. *Cock o' the North* was allocated to York throughout the 1950s except for a brief loan to Neville Hill and was withdrawn in February 1960.

The Big 4-6-2Ts

Saltburn-allocated 'A8' 4-6-2T No. 69869 waits at Darlington Bank Top with a train to Saltburn on 31st August 1952. These big tanks had been produced between 1931 and 1936 by rebuilding the North Eastern Railway Raven Class 'D' (L&NER Class 'H1') 4-4-4Ts and were ideal for handling heavy secondary passenger traffic beyond the capabilities of the NER 'G5' 0-4-4Ts. The decision to rebuild them followed the allocation of newly built Robinson 'A5' tanks to the area which had demonstrated the advantages of a six-coupled tank over the poor riding 'H1's. During the process of rebuilding, they were modified to allow the 'A8' boiler to be interchangeable with those of the 'A6', 'A7', 'A8', 'H1', and 'T1' classes. No. 69869, which has the early type '63A' boiler with the cladding flush with the smokebox, remained at Saltburn from January 1950 until February 1958, thereafter working off Middlesbrough and Thornaby. The inevitable end came in June 1960, Darlington Works immediately cutting it up.

'A8' 4-6-2T No. 69892 at Darlington Bank Top, probably with a Saltburn train, on 11th August 1956. It was allocated to Saltburn from 1946 until November 1957 when it was transferred to West Hartlepool where it stayed for just one year. An 'A5/2' 4-6-2T is in the background where there is lots of activity loading the brake van. Thirteen of these, based on the Great Central Robinson 'A5' 4-6-2T but with reduced height boiler mountings, improved cabs and other detail differences, were built in 1925/6 for service in the North East and although they subsequently moved away, most returned to the area in the early 1950s. Amongst other duties, they shared the working of the trains from Darlington to Richmond with 'L1' 2-6-4Ts and to Saltburn with the 'A8's.

The 'cage' type bunker of 'A8' 4-6-2T No. 69869 shows up well as it arrives at Bank Top from Saltburn on 11th August 1956. On the left behind the cattle wagons is the Cleveland Bridge & Engineering Co. Ltd works which has since been demolished and replaced by a housing estate and Territorial Army centre. The company was responsible for building some well-known local bridges including the Middlesbrough Transporter Bridge and the Edward VII bridge in Newcastle. Overseas, it manufactured the Victoria Falls Bridge and was involved in the construction of the Sydney Harbour Bridge with Dorman Long. The two companies merged in 1990 after both had been taken over after the Second World War. Note the cranes in the right background at the far end of the extensive yard.

Shunters and station pilots

One of a large number of ex-War Department 0-6-0STs allocated to Darlington during the 1950s, 'J94' No. 68043 makes its way past the station in 1952 with a a very long trip freight. It had been built at Vulcan Foundry in 1945 and was at Darlington from July 1949 until withdrawn in May 1965; No. 68043 was not one of the class fitted with an extended bunker.

With the massive thermometer on the Heating & Air Conditioning Company factory showing 68 degrees, 'J71' 0-6-0T No. 68239 is on shunting duty at Darlington on 10th August 1956. It was one of the 120-strong class built as NER No. 494 in 1887 and was renumbered to No. 8239 in 1946. They were superseded by the more powerful 'J72' class, with smaller wheels and larger cylinders, which continued to be built under British Railways.

'J94' 0-6-0ST No. 68010 at the north end of the station in the early 1960s had been built by Hunslet in 1944 as WD No. 75117. The class was a simplified version for the War Department of the company's '50550' saddle tank and the L&NER bought seventy-five of them after the end of World War Two. No. 68010, which had been fitted with an extended bunker and rear cab windows in 1949, was transferred from Blaydon to Darlington in September 1961 and was withdrawn from there in May 1965. The DMU depot, which was completed in 1957 on the site of former carriage sidings, is visible in the distance behind the North signal box; the 150-lever box was built in 1923. The coal-fired power station in the centre background had been rebuilt on the site in 1940 and had three large hyperboloid reinforced concrete cooling towers and three brick-built chimneys, with a generating capacity of 57 megawatts. It was closed in October 1976 and the cooling towers were demolished in 1979. The extensive Haughton Road sidings are in the right background.

L&NER-built 'J50' 0-6-0T No. 68934 on a trip working from the Haughton Road sidings a short distance north of the station. No. 68934 was transferred to Darlington from Low Moor in March 1958 and was there for almost eighteen months before moving to Ardsley in August 1959 for its last four years in service.

The station pilots at Darlington were replaced in the early 1960s by 204bhp diesel shunters, later classified as '04' but never carrying TOPS numbers. No. D2318 had been built at Darlington Works with parts supplied by the Drewry Car Company Ltd. and entered service in March 1961. Allocated to Darlington throughout, No. D2318 had a very short working life and was withdrawn in February 1968 and sold for scrap to Hughes Bolckow (part of the T.W. Ward Group) at Blyth in May.

CHAPTER 2 - DARLINGTON

No. 60114 waits in the autumn sunshine before departure with a northbound express on 25th September 1960. It was the first Peppercorn 'A1' Pacific and was completed at Doncaster in August 1948. The 'A1' was an enlarged version of the 'A2', sharing the same boiler but with 6ft 9ins driving wheels compared with 6ft 2ins. No. 60114 was named *W.P. Allen* six months after it entered traffic and was withdrawn in December 1964 from Doncaster shed, where it had been allocated since late 1957. The snap-head rivets on the tender were used by Doncaster but the Darlington-built 'A1's had the more expensive flush rivets.

A LM&SR thorn between two L&NER roses in 1961, but the only one of the three to escape the cutter's torch, Brighton-built Fairburn Class '4' 2-6-4T No. 42085 is now preserved at the Lakeside & Haverthwaite Railway. No. 42085 was first allocated to Brighton in February 1951 and moved later in the same year to Stewarts Lane. In March 1952 it was transferred to Heaton and in July of that year to Darlington. Scarborough followed in 1955; Whitby and Manningham in 1956; Whitby again in 1958, York in 1959 and Darlington in 1961. 'A4' No. 60006 *Sir Ralph Wedgwood* went to Scotland in October 1963 and was withdrawn two years later. Peppercorn 'A1' No. 60127 *Wilson Worsdell* had been a Heaton engine from new until sent to Tweedmouth in September 1962. It was to stay there until October 1964, and was withdrawn from its final shed, Gateshead, in June 1965.

The driver of No. 60539 *Bronzino* looks back observing the loading of the parcels van of his train. No. 60539 was the last of the Peppercorn 'A2' Pacifics, emerging from Doncaster in August 1948 as their works number 2030. This picture was taken while it was allocated to Heaton where it stayed until late 1961 when it too moved to Tweedmouth. No. 60539 was condemned from there in November of the following year. Very unusually, the two oil headlamps have their covers loose and one has flapped open.

Freight and parcels

'A1' No. 60155 *Borderer* with a northbound freight near the end of its days. It was allocated to York for its last three years in traffic and was withdrawn in October 1965. No. 60155 was one of the five 'A1's built with roller-bearing axleboxes and the first to reach one million miles. The bearing sets were expensive, costing an additional £3,000 per engine, but were justified by the increased mileage achieved between repairs. The cantilevered section of the North signal box to improve sighting on the east side can be seen in this photograph.

The now-preserved 'Q6' 0-8-0 No. 63395 runs through Darlington on a mixed freight with six Conflat 'L' wagons at the front, each carrying three containers which would have contained bulk dry powders. No. 63395, which was built by the NER in December 1918, was allocated to Darlington between June 1959 and in December 1963 when it moved to Consett. It was the final 'Q6' to be overhauled at Darlington Works, in September 1965, and was one of the last two 'Q6's in service. Following withdrawal in September 1967, No. 63395 was purchased by the North Eastern Locomotive Preservation Group in April 1968 and has been based on the North Yorkshire Moors Railway where it returned to service in 2016.

Named 'B1' 4-6-0 No. 61037 *Jairou* with a parcels train departing south from Darlington on 29th October 1962. It had been transferred from Thornaby to Darlington in June 1959 and was withdrawn from there in May 1964.

Foreigners

Near the end of steam on the North Eastern Region, a number of ex-LM&SR tank engines arrived in the north east to take over from former L&NER locomotives which had been withdrawn. Three Fairburn 2-6-4Ts had been there in the early 1950s and several of the Stanier version arrived in the 1960s, together with at least one Fowler 2-6-4T. No. 42405 was allocated to Darlington for its last three years, from November 1962 to October 1965 when it was withdrawn. The Fowler and Fairburn tanks were used on the remaining local services, such as those to Crook, which had not yet been dieselised.

WD 'Austerity' 2-8-0 No. 90348 was a magnet for the cameras when it was used to take the RCTS 'East Midlander No. 5' railtour from Bank Top to North Road Works on 13th May 1962 after the train had arrived in Darlington from Nottingham behind Southern 'Schools' No. 30925 Cheltenham and LM&SR '2P' 4-4-0 No. 40646. The 'Austerities' were only ever this clean when they were repainted during works visits!

No. 30925 Cheltenham, No. 40646 and some of the members of the RCTS tour party pose for the cameramen before it returns to Nottingham from Darlington with the RCTS railtour on 13th May 1962. The 'Schools' was chosen by the RCTS for several of its railtours, in recognition of the Society's founding at Cheltenham in 1927 and a drawing of No. 30925 appeared on the front cover of its monthly magazine, The Railway Observer, for many years.

Diesel multiple units

Two Metropolitan-Cammell four-car sets form a peak-hour train to Saltburn in 1957 with 'A2' No. 60517 *Ocean Swell* in the background. Later Class '101', they were the first diesel multiple units delivered to Darlington and were mainly used on the Saltburn services which ran every half-hour. The thirteen sets entered service in August 1957 after the Darlington DMU depot had been completed.

By the end of 1958, steam had been swept away from most of the local passenger and branch services originating from Darlington as this picture shows with four Metropolitan-Cammell units waiting in the station where only a couple of years earlier the 'A8' and 'A5' 4-6-2Ts would have been standing. The Richmond and Saltburn services were the first to be dieselised, in August 1957, followed the next month by those to Crook and Middleton-in-Teesdale and in February 1958 the Darlington-Penrith service.

Main line diesels

English Electric Type '4' No. D285 with a train of containers passes through Darlington on 25th September 1960. Note the old style running-in board lit by no less than eight individual lamps, and the early 1930s colour light signals.

The driver of Class '46' No. D175 waits for departure time on 25th May 1968 with the 08.31 Darlington-Stockton section of the Stephenson Locomotive Society's 'Flying Scotsman' Pullman railtour to Inverkeithing; the 'A3' took the train from Stockton to Inverkeithing and back, assisted on the return from Newcastle by 'Deltic' No. D9007 *Pinza*.

North Road station

Although the Stockton & Darlington Railway had a station in Darlington at North Road from 1825, the present station dates from the 1842 although the North Eastern Railway modernised it in the 1890s. The station is close to Bank Top and only served the local community, resulting in the first proposals for closure back in the 1930s. However, it hung on, somehow surviving the Beeching axe in 1963. It was reduced to a single platform after closure of the Middleton-in-Teesdale Branch in November 1964 and remains in use today serving the Bishop Auckland line trains. As an unstaffed halt it suffered vandalism until the local Council and interested parties formed The Darlington Railway Centre and Museum in 1973 utilising the original platforms, train shed, offices and station building. Main line trains continued to use the single platform which was partitioned off.

One of a pair of BR Standard Class '3' 2-6-2Ts allocated to Darlington when new in December 1954, No. 82028 was passing the Whessoe Foundry approaching North Road station with a train from Barnard Castle in 1955. No. 82028 remained at Darlington until September 1958 when it was transferred to Scarborough.

One of the ex-War Department 0-6-0STs allocated to Darlington in the 1950s, No. 68025 was shunting the extensive sidings near Darlington North Road on 25th August 1956. It was built by Hudswell, Clarke in 1944 as WD No. 71498. After purchase by the L&NER in June 1946 it became No. 8025. No. 68025 remained at Darlington until withdrawn in 1963.

Viewed from the west end nearest the Works, the track on the left is still in use for the Bishop Auckland service. The island platform is partitioned off to form the Darlington Railway Centre and Museum, now branded as 'The Head of Steam' by Darlington Borough Council.

The second of the two BR Standard Class '3' 2-6-2Ts allocated to Darlington when new in December 1954, No. 82029 waits to leave Darlington North Road on 25th August 1956 with a train to Penrith. They were used mainly on the Darlington-Penrith trains until DMUs took these over in January 1958. No. 82029 remained at Darlington until January 1958 when it was transferred to West Hartlepool. It left the North Eastern Region from Malton for the Southern Region in 1963 and was withdrawn from Nine Elms when steam ended there on 9th July 1967.

Works

Darlington Works was opened in 1854 by the Stockton & Darlington Railway, replacing its original facility at Shildon. It was situated close to North Road station and expanded over the years between 1867 and 1912. The 1923 Grouping had little effect on the Works and it continued to build new locomotives well into nationalisation days with both BR Standard classes and then diesels. The last new locomotive was built in August 1964 and the Works closed in April 1966.

Under construction and newly built

Darlington Works built all of the BR Standard Class '2' 2-6-0s, sixty-five in total, over a period of four years starting in December 1952. The engines were based on the LM&SR Ivatt Class '2' design, tinkered with for the sake of standardisation on the nationalised railway. This picture shows two of the engines newly completed, one in primer and the one further away in its first coat of black gloss. In the background is 'D49' 4-4-0 No. 62709 *Berwickshire* which was in the Works during May 1954 meaning that these engines are two of the three from Nos. 78022-78024.

Darlington-built sixty-five BR Sulzer Type '2' (later Class '25') diesels between April 1961 and August 1964, Nos. D5151-D5185, D5223-D5232 and D7578-D7597, the latter being the last locomotive built at the works. No. D7584 was nearing completion in January 1964 and was delivered to Toton the following month. It had a twenty year working life and was withdrawn as No. 25234 in November 1984.

Newly delivered to Darlington from the North British Locomotive Company in Glasgow on 7th July 1953, No. 11700 the first of the diesel-hydraulic 0-4-0 shunters built for British Railways. It went officially into traffic on 25th July and was allocated to West Hartlepool; it was renumbered as No. D2700 in Darlington Works February 1958 after initially being given the incorrect number D2600. The design was particularly unsuccessful, and this locomotive spent long periods of its ten-year working life in store; it was reported as lying out of use behind the old Paint Shop at Darlington Stooperdale Works from August 1955 until 1958. It ended with the dubious distinction of being the first 'D'-numbered locomotive to be withdrawn when it was finally taken out of service in October 1964, having been stored since the previous November, and was cut-up at Darlington Works.

An altogether more successful design of diesel shunter was the BR standard 350bhp diesel-electric 0-6-0 based on the LM&SR design which had been developed over two decades. Darlington Works built 411 examples, one-third of the class, starting with No. 13060 in August 1953 and ending with No. D4192 in 1962. No. 13149 was built there in 1955 and went into traffic on 21st July. It was allocated to Newport shed on Teesside, moving to Darlington in 1956 and then to Thornaby in 1958 and became No. D3149 in September 1959. No. D3149 was an early withdrawal, in July 1970, as one of a number of the class fitted with Lister-Blackstone engines and GEC traction motors rather than the classic English Electric EE6KT engines and traction motors. This rendered them non-standard as British Rail attempted to reduce the large number of different types in its diesel fleet under the 1968 National Traction Plan.

Outside

Incredibly, twenty-eight 'J72' 0-6-0Ts were built by British Railways between 1949 and 1951, over half-a-century after the last ones had been built by the North Eastern Railway. Apparently, it had been included by A.H. Peppercorn as the L&NER standard light shunting engine filling the gap for an unspecified design included in his predecessor's standardisation plans. No. 69017 was built at Darlington in January 1950 and was a works shunter on 3rd June in that year. It was initially allocated to Darlington until 11th June 1950 when it moved to Borough Gardens, the freight shed near Gateshead.

The L&NER purchased over fifty vertically boilered, geared shunters from the Sentinel company between 1927 and 1931 and they were maintained at Darlington. This one was built as L&NER No. 174 and Sentinel Works No. 7845 in 1929, was renumbered as No. 848 in 1946 and became British Railways No. 68148. On 19th August 1951 at Darlington Works, it was ready to return to its home shed at Bridlington where it would have been used to shunt the local yards, positioning wagons in advance of the daily freight, thereby reducing the time needed to shunt the yard by the main line engine, a practice adopted by the L&NER in the 1930s.

Neasden's 'L1' 2-6-4T No. 67762 outside the Stripping shed in the 1950s. It was built by the North British Locomotive Company, entering service in January 1949 and spent most of the 1950s at the former Great Central Railway shed, working local trains out of Marylebone. No. 67762 had three years at Colwick before withdrawal in October 1961.

One of the six 'A4' Pacifics preserved, No. 60009 *Union of South Africa* minus its front-end streamlined casings. It was in Darlington Works for a Light Casual repair arriving on 5th February 1964 and leaving on 18th April. It had been allocated to Aberdeen Ferryhill since mid-1962 and was a regular on the 3-hour expresses from Glasgow. No. 60009 was withdrawn in 1966 and purchased for preservation by John Cameron who ran it on the Lochty Private Railway for several years. It has since operated regularly on the main line.

One of the first Class '45' BR Sulzer Type '4s' No. D14 in the Works on 8th June 1963. It was built at Derby in late 1960 and has a 55H Leeds Neville Hill shedplate on the left-hand nose door, although records show it had been transferred from there to Holbeck in December 1962. It has split headcode boxes on either side of the connecting doors which show up well here. The fitting of these doors was quickly discontinued at Derby (and never featured in Crewe's production). They were sealed up and later removed as this early batch, Nos. D11-D15, made Works visits for Classified repairs.

Three North Eastern Railway-built 'J72s' were on the scrap line awaiting their fate on 13th May 1962. Nearest the camera is No. 68729, then No. 68688, both withdrawn from Thornaby in October 1961, and furthest away No. 68703 withdrawn from West Hartlepool also in October 1961. The scrapyard was located on the opposite side of the former Stockton & Darlington Railway main line to the works, adjacent to North Road station. It is now a recreation ground and car park for the museum.

Inside

No. 26500 was one of two identical 'ES1' Bo-Bo electric locomotives built for the North Eastern Railway by Brush Traction to work freight over the ¾ mile long, horseshoe-shaped line between Trafalgar Yard in Manors and Newcastle Quayside Yard which had gradients up to 1 in 27 and three tunnels. They began operation on the newly electrified line in 1905 and the two locomotives worked there until it was de-electrified in 1964 and they were withdrawn. No. 26500 was preserved and is currently at the NRM Shildon museum.

Top
No. 26500 is jacked up and off its wheels in Darlington Works in late 1951.

Middle
No. 26500 has been put back together and is now in the weigh-house.

Lower
No. 26500 outside the Erecting Shop, ready to return to Tyneside.

CHAPTER 2 - DARLINGTON

The first Doncaster-built Ivatt '4MT' 2-6-0 No. 43051 inside the paint shop during a General repair from 18th May 1961 to 12th August during which it was fitted with AWS. Repairs to the Eastern Region and North Eastern Region members of the class had been transferred to Darlington from Doncaster at the start of 1959. No. 43051 stayed on the NER from new in 1950 until withdrawn in January 1967; at the date of this picture it was allocated to Neville Hill.

'A3' No. 60052 *Prince Palatine* in the Erecting Shop during April 1965 when it was undergoing a 'Light Casual' repair from 19th March until 11th May. Its nameplate is still in place but the Doncaster worksplate has gone missing.

Shed

Darlington shed, coded 51A after nationalisation, comprised a double-ended seven-road running shed completed in October 1940 with an adjoining two-road repair shop and a 19th Century eighteen-road roundhouse around a 45ft turntable, which was mainly used for tank engines. Its facilities included a 70ft vacuum-operated turntable and a mechanical coaling tower, both built during the 1939/40 modernisation. Its own allocation consisted mainly of tank and freight engines but engines newly built or repaired at the nearby Works could always be found there whilst running-in. In the first half of the 1950s there was a preponderance of 'B1' 4-6-0s, 'K1' 2-6-0s, ex-GCR 'A5' 4-6-2Ts, 'J94' 0-6-0STs and 'J21'/'J25' 0-6-0s. One of the features of the shed's allocation was the high turnover of several classes: between 1957 and 1964 there were thirty-two different 'B1' 4-6-0s, thirty-one 'J94's and thirty 'Austerity' 2-8-0s. The shed closed on 26th March 1966, a week before the Works shut down.

Early 1950s

As anyone who lived close to a steam shed could confirm, raising steam could be a messy business as demonstrated by Peppercorn 'K1' 2-6-0 No. 62047 at Darlington shed on 3rd June 1950. It had been built by the North British Locomotive Company in October 1949 and was allocated to Darlington until June 1956 when it moved to York, although it returned to Darlington in 1958 for a short spell.

Below: Worsdell 'J25' 0-6-0 No. 65706 at Darlington soon after it was renumbered in November 1948 and while it was allocated to West Auckland shed for working over the Pennines to Penrith and Tebay. It moved to North and South Blyth for its last four years of service and was withdrawn at the end of 1959 before being cut up at Darlington. Note the footplate is distorted. Buckling of the footplate over the front draw hook would suggest that a heavy impact had occurred to the right front buffer. This would account for the aforementioned damage and the lifting of the right-hand side footplate and angle iron between buffer beam and leading wheel.

Worsdell 'G5' 0-4-4T No. 67284 outside the roundhouse on 9th June 1953. It was a Darlington engine from the end of 1950 until withdrawn in October 1956. Darlington generally had three of these engines on its books and they were used on the Middleton-in-Teesdale railmotor service.

'D49/2' 4-4-0 No. 62775 *The Tynedale* at Darlington in 1955 was one of the engines built with Lentz Rotary cam poppet valves. It was allocated to Leeds Neville Hill until October 1956 when it was transferred to Selby. Although the last of the 'Hunts' to enter traffic, emerging from Darlington Works in February 1935, it was withdrawn at the end of 1958.

With the Haughton Road power station in the background, Raven 'Q7' 0-8-0 No. 63461 from Blaydon shed where it was allocated between June 1956 and June 1957. It was then transferred to Tyne Dock, staying there until the end of 1962. It met its end at Darlington Works in March 1963.

Fresh from the Works, WD 2-8-0 No. 90462 in 1954, is temporarily a vision in shiny black which would not last for long. It was allocated to Newport from 1949 until the shed closed in 1958 and it moved across to the new depot at Thornaby.

CHAPTER 2 - DARLINGTON

Tank variety

'L1' 2-6-4T No. 67750 with a bunker full of slack coal on 25th September 1960. No. 67750 was one of three built by the North British Locomotive Company and entered traffic in December 1948 allocated from new to Darlington, where it stayed until the end of 1961. The 'L1's were used on the Saltburn and Richmond trains alongside the 4-6-2Ts.

On the same day, one of Darlington's extensive stud of 'J94' 0-6-0STs, No. 68025, was on shed. It had been at Darlington since before nationalisation and was withdrawn from there in October 1963. Built by Hudswell, Clarke for the War Department in 1944, it was one of seventy-five purchased by the L&NER in 1946. They were a simplified version of the standard Hunslet 18in. inside cylinder industrial 0-6-0ST, reducing the number of steel castings by using cast iron wheel centres and slide valves, and welded steel plate frames. Two of them had their coal bunkers extended in 1947 and No. 68025 was similarly modified in November 1949 with an extended bunker, ladder, steps, and rear cab windows; others were also modified but many remained in their original condition until withdrawn.

After nationalisation in 1948 the LM&SR Fairburn Class '4' 2-6-4Ts were produced for other BR Regions. No. 42084 was built at Brighton in February 1951 for the Southern Region but moved to the North Eastern Region in early 1952. The NER was waiting for delivery of three new BR Standard 2-6-4Ts and to fill the gap, three Fairburn 2-6-4Ts, Nos. 42083-42085, were transferred in their place. They were put to work immediately on the Middlesbrough-Newcastle fast hourly services. No. 42084 went initially to Middlesbrough in March and then on to Darlington a month later where it was photographed, probably in 1953. No. 42084 stayed there until 1955 when it was transferred to Scarborough. The position of the central lamp irons half-way down the smokebox front is a souvenir of its days on the Southern. Although at first glance No. 42084 is virtually identical with the earlier Stanier engines, close study of No. 42639 below shows a number of differences. Most obvious are the more utilitarian open front footplating, fluted coupling rods and the snap-head rivets on the tanks; less noticeable is the shorter wheelbase and the open footsteps.

Stanier 2-6-4T No. 42639 was at several North Eastern Region sheds during the 1950s and arrived at Darlington in November 1961 following withdrawal of the shed's 'L1's. It was one of four LM&SR-designed 2-6-4Ts which replaced them, the others being Stanier Nos. 42477 and 42553 and Fairburn No. 42085. The curved front footplate, filled-in front steps and plain section coupling rods show up well, as does the AWS protection plate which dated from the fitting of the equipment in February 1961. No. 42639 was at 51A until June 1964 when it was transferred to Ardsley.

Mixed traffic

'V2' 2-6-2 No. 60901 leaves the shed on 25th August 1962 when it was allocated to Thornaby. No. 60901 was built at Darlington in 1940 as L&NER No. 4872, becoming No. 901 in November 1946. It is paired with a flush-riveted 4,200 gallon 'Group Standard' tender, the type built with the class.

Peppercorn 'K1' 2-6-0 62045 with a classmate behind on 11th May 1963. Throughout the 1950s and up to 1963, Darlington had at least ten of the class on its books and one of their main tasks was the working of freight trains originating at Darlington which they shared with the shed's 'B1' 4-6-0s.

Pacific Pilots

A long tradition of main line standby pilots at Darlington dated back to May 1928 when the non-stop 'Flying Scotsman' was introduced. At nationalisation and until August 1948 the duty was shared between two 'V2' 2-6-2s and two NER 'C7' Atlantics. When the latter were withdrawn they were replaced by 'A3' Pacifics. The first pair of these were Nos 60070 and 60076 which were transferred from Gateshead to Darlington. From then until November 1964 a different pair of Gateshead 'A3's took over, at roughly six-monthly intervals, one covering the northbound and the other the southbound workings. The standby engines were kept permanently in steam, apart from routine boiler wash-outs, etc. and one was usually to be found on or near the turntable. The pilots usually only worked as far as York to the south and Newcastle to the north, but occasionally did reach Edinburgh or King's Cross.

No. 60076 *Galopin* was one of the first pair of 'A3's transferred from Gateshead and subsequently returned for four more stints including February to June 1956, during which time this picture was taken.

Double-chimneyed 'A3' No. 60052 *Prince Palatine* on 25th September 1960. This was its first period as a Darlington standby, having been transferred from Gateshead in June 1960, and it returned for a second time in December 1962. The 1924-built engine was the last 'A3' to remain in service when it was withdrawn in January 1966. It had been rebuilt from an 'A1' in 1941 and had a double chimney from November 1958.

No. 60091 *Captain Cuttle* awaits the call to action on 13th May 1962. It was near the end of its second spell on standby, returning to Gateshead in June. No. 60091 was fitted with a double chimney in March 1959, German-style smoke deflectors in October 1961 and was withdrawn in October 1964. Its tender has a rare example of a post-1956 British Railways crest with forward facing lion on the right-hand side. There were right- and left-handed versions of this crest transfer so the lion could face forward no matter on which side of the tender it was placed, but after complaints from the College of Arms all lions faced left.

'A1' No. 60124 *Kenilworth*, waiting by the turntable in 1965, was transferred from York once the last 'A3' pilots had gone in November 1964 and continued in the role until March 1966. It was joined in January 1966 by No. 60145 *Saint Mungo* which arrived from York in exchange for Darlington's last 'V2' No. 60806 and was withdrawn in June of that year.

Haughton Road

'V2' 2-6-2 No.60806 with a southbound freight passing the DMU depot on 17th July 1965 as a 'Peak' heads north. It had been transferred to Darlington in August 1964 from West Hartlepool. A 'Pulverite' wagon from the Standard Pulverised Fuel Co. Ltd leads the train. This was built by Charles Roberts in 1937 and originally worked from Brancepeth Colliery to an unknown industrial customer. In the process pulverised coal is entrained into a stream of air and 'flash burned'. It burns efficiently and quickly because the particles are very small, and therefore has a high surface area to volume ratio, giving lots of exposure to the oxygen necessary for combustion. Note the quality of the trackwork in the yard.

BR Sulzer Type '2' No. D5234 heads a southbound Class '4' fitted freight which is about to pass under Haughton Road bridge, probably in 1964. It was the second of the class to be built with a re-styled cab omitting the rarely used gangway doors of the earlier locomotives. The position of the air intakes was also changed, and the locomotives had a two-tone green livery similar to that used on the Brush Type '4'. No. D5234 was built in December 1963 and was on the LMR Midland Division for its first ten years. It became No. 25084 in 1974 and worked until December 1983. On the left of the train is the Albert Hill Foundry of the Darlington Forge Company Limited which was closed in 1967.

3 – Northwards from Darlington

The first line from Darlington to Newcastle was George Hudson's Newcastle & Darlington Junction Railway which opened in 1844. In his characteristic style, he cobbled together several lines already in existence and ended up with a route via Ferryhill, Leamside and Pelaw to Gateshead. Utilising this line as far as Ferryhill, the North Eastern Railway opened what is today's East Coast main line route to Durham at the end of 1871. The 'Old Main Line' continued as an important freight and diversionary route and also formed the southern half of the branch from Durham to Sunderland with a regular passenger service which continued up to 1964.

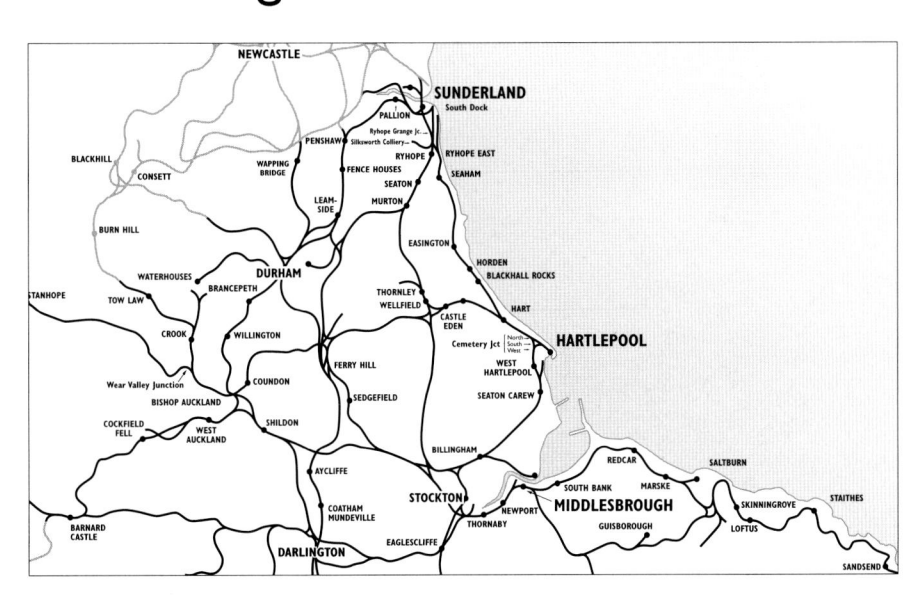

The East Coast main line to Durham

Coatham Mundeville

'B1' 4-6-0 No. 61051 with a northbound train of empty hoppers has just passed a Pacific-hauled southbound express at Coatham Mundeville near Darlington in April 1961. It was built for the L&NER by the North British Locomotive Company in June 1946 and was allocated to Darnall shed at Sheffield from 1956 until 1963 when it moved to nearby Canklow. The Up track has been re-laid with concrete sleepers but the Down line still retains wooden sleepers.

'Deltic' No. D9009 *Alycidon* sweeps round the curve at Coatham Mundeville with the King's Cross-Edinburgh 'Heart of Midlothian' on 23rd May 1964. Following in the East Coast tradition of naming its express locomotives after racehorses, No. D9009 was named after the horse that won the Ascot Gold Cup in 1949.

Ketton Lane overbridge Aycliffe

Passing under Ketton Lane overbridge at Aycliffe, BR Sulzer Type '4' No. D12 was working a southbound express to the Western Region from Newcastle in 1963. Built in October 1960, it was the second of the uprated 'Peaks' from Derby and the first five of this batch continued the use of the nose-end gangway doors fitted to Nos. D1-D10. These were soon discontinued at Derby, and never featured in Crewe's production of the class, and the doors were soon removed. No. D12 became No. 45011 under TOPS and was withdrawn in 1981.

The final fifty-six BR Sulzer Type '4's were fitted with Brush traction motors instead of the Crompton Parkinson type used on the Class '45', and hence became Class '46' under TOPS. No. D180 which was working a southbound cattle train in 1963 shows the modified front end of the later 'Peaks' with a single headcode box. Note also the cast iron 52A shed plate below the headcode box. No. D180 entered traffic in September 1962 and was allocated to Gateshead through until withdrawal in November 1980 as No. 46043.

CHAPTER 3 - NORTHWARDS FROM DARLINGTON

'Deltic' No. D9019 with the Up 'Queen of Scots' Pullman from Glasgow Queen Street to King's Cross in 1963. It was the last of the class to be named, receiving the name *Royal Highland Fusilier* in a ceremony at Glasgow Central station in September 1965. After withdrawal in December 1981 as No. 55019, it was purchased by the Deltic Preservation Society and is currently (2019) working main line railtours. The all-Pullman train includes a wooden-bodied Brake Second at the front of the Mark 1 Pullman cars; no Mark 1 Pullman brakes were produced. The Second Class Pullman coaches were numbered but only the First Class coaches had names. The 'Queen of Scots' was replaced at the start of the Summer 1964 timetable by the 'White Rose Pullman' running only as far north as Leeds, reflecting a decline in passengers using the train further north.

English Electric Type '4' No. D278 in 1963 heads the block cement empties from Uddingston near Glasgow to Cliffe in Kent back to the works owned by Associated Portland Cement Manufacturing (Blue Circle). The train was worked between Kent and York by a pair of BRC&W Type '3's where the motive power was changed. No. D278 was allocated to York from November 1961 until March 1967 and remained on the North Eastern until withdrawn as No. 40078 in August 1981.

The first of the English Electric Type '4's to be built with a single four-character headcode panel, No. D345 with a southbound parcels train in 1963. It was at York from June 1963 until the end of 1967, and after withdrawal in 1983 as No. 40145 it was purchased by the Class 40 Preservation Society and has worked again on the main line for many years although it is currently (2019) under overhaul at Barrow Hill.

During the first week of its brief spell in ordinary passenger service, No. HS4000 *Kestrel* heads the 07.55 King's Cross-Newcastle near Aycliffe on 23rd October 1969. The 4,000bhp single-engined Brush prototype was completed in late 1967 and given a striking two-tone golden yellow/chocolate brown livery scheme. After several months of testing, it then spent the next twelve months mainly on freight work because its axle load was excessive for use on passenger trains. *Kestrel* was fitted with new Class '47' type bogies in mid-1969 to reduce its weight and to allow it to be used on high-speed passenger work.

Blue-liveried English Electric Type '3' No. 6794 with a southbound train of Presflos in October 1972, with Brafferton village in the distance. It had been transferred to Thornaby from Hull Dairycoates a year earlier and became No. 37094 in November 1973. It was refurbished at the end of 1988 with re-geared bogies, additional ballast weights and the main generator replaced by an alternator, becoming No. 37716. After a period in store, it went to Spain in 2001 as one of the Special Projects locomotives used on the construction of a high-speed line and then went back into store at Dollands Moor. It was sold in 2013 by DB Schenker to Direct Rail Services based at Carlisle Kingmoor where it is employed mainly on Nuclear Traffic.

Ferryhill

Gateshead 'Deltic' No. D9002 *The King's Own Yorkshire Light Infantry* with the 2pm King's Cross to Edinburgh at Ferryhill on 9th May 1964. It had been named at York on 4th April 1963, the name having previously been carried by 'V2' 2-6-2 No. 60872 and was the first of the class to be repainted into BR Corporate Blue, in October 1966. It received TOPS No. 55002 in December 1973 and was in service until 2nd January 1982, specially repainted in two-tone green for its last year in traffic, after which it was preserved in the National Collection and is currently a non-working exhibit.

CHAPTER 3 - NORTHWARDS FROM DARLINGTON

Darlington-Durham via Shildon and Bishop Auckland

The secondary route between Darlington and Durham via Shildon and Bishop Auckland was opened in two stages. In 1843 the Stockton & Darlington Railway completed an extension to Bishop Auckland and the section north to Durham was opened in 1856. The main objective was to serve the collieries in the area, but a local passenger service began in 1857 and the line was occasionally used as a diversionary route when there were engineering works on the East Coast main line between Darlington and Durham.

Shildon

Metropolitan-Cammell two-car DMU with No. E56067 leading departs from Shildon with a service to Richmond on 17th June 1961. It was one of the sets originally built for the Hull area in 1957 and subsequently transferred to South Gosforth and then on to Darlington.

BR Standard Class '3' 2-6-0 No. 77002 emerges from the southern end of Shildon Tunnel on 14th June 1962. It had been at West Auckland since July 1954 and was there until the end of 1962 when it was transferred to Darlington. No. 77002 was on the Black Boy Branch, a short 2½ mile long line which left the former Stockton & Darlington line at Shildon to serve the collieries in the Dene Valley.

It's a Sunday so this was a day of rest for the six BR Sulzer Type '2's and a 204bhp shunter in the background. On the right are rows of 16T mineral wagons and coal hoppers. On 19th September 1965 'A4' No. 60004 *William Whitelaw* had brought the RCTS West Riding branch 'Blyth & Tyne' railtour from Leeds to Eaglesclifffe and picked it up again at Darlington North Road to take it via Shildon, Bishop Auckland and Durham to Newcastle. The 'A4' had been specially requested by the organisers and No. 60004, one of the eight remaining members of the class which were all allocated to Aberdeen Ferryhill, had to be worked down for the tour. It had been built in 1937 as No. 4462 *Great Snipe* but was renamed in July 1941.

William Whitelaw is about to pass through Shildon station and take the right-hand fork towards Bishop Auckland, the left fork going to West Auckland and Barnard Castle after passing the extensive wagon works at Shildon.

Bishop Auckland

Looking north at the Durham platforms on 12th August 1953. The train on the right headed by 'A8' 4-6-2T No. 69851 is the 2.2pm from Sunderland to Middleton-in-Teesdale via Durham, Bishop Auckland and Barnard Castle. *Walter Dendy/B.W. Brooksbank collection*

Willington

North Eastern Railway 1894 built 'G5' 0-4-4T No. 67248 pauses at Willington with a Sunderland-Durham-Bishop Auckland service in April 1957. It had been transferred to Durham from Blaydon in July 1952 and stayed there until the end of 1957 when it moved to Malton for its final year in traffic.

Brancepeth

No. 67248, probably on the same day as in the picture on the previous page, waits at Brancepeth. The line between Bishop Auckland and Durham opened to freight in 1856 and to passengers the following year with intermediate stations at Hunwick, Willington and Brancepeth. The Sunderland-Durham-Bishop Auckland passenger service ended in May 1964 and the line was closed completely in 1968.

Durham

The current station at Durham was originally just an intermediate stop on the Bishop Auckland Branch from Leamside. It was opened in 1857 but major improvements were made in 1871/2 for the new direct East Coast main line from Ferryhill. The station was widened to provide two through platforms and bays for local services. Of these, the Lanchester Valley service to Blackhill closed in 1939 and the branch service to Waterhouses ended in 1951. The Bishop Auckland and Sunderland trains were withdrawn in May 1964, leaving Durham as a through main line station only.

The Sunday morning pedestrians walking up North Road don't give a second glance to 'A1' No. 60124 *H.A. Ivatt* as it passes overhead on 4th September 1955. The station approach road was to the left of Lynchs' [sic] Radio Ltd, stockist of the now long-defunct 'Ekco' and 'Philco' brands, and the Station Hotel is on the right before the viaduct.

'9F' 2-10-0 No. 92042 passes over the rooftops on the approach to Durham station with a northbound Class 'D' express freight on 16th July 1960. It was at Peterborough's New England shed from new in January 1955 until June 1963 when it moved to Colwick.

The penultimate 'A4' No. 60033 *Seagull* ready to depart with a northbound express in the mid-1950s. Like *Mallard*, it was built with a double chimney which led to it being chosen to represent the class in the 1948 Locomotive Exchanges. It did not cover itself in glory and was failed with an overheated big-end when working on the Southern Region, and was replaced by *Mallard* which then suffered the same problem. In the background is Durham Cathedral, completed in 1133, and now a World Heritage site. Its Norman architecture has survived largely intact, except for the addition of two chapels and the 216ft high central tower which dates back to 1484, and which was re-opened to the public in 2019 following a three-year renovation project.

'G5' 0-4-4T No. 67248 from Sunderland shed waits to depart from the south bay with a train to Bishop Auckland. The passenger service over the line from Durham ceased in May 1964 although the line remained open for another four years. No. 67248 was built as NER No. 1869 in August 1894 and became L&NER No. 7248 under the 1946 renumbering scheme and No. 67248 in October 1948. It was withdrawn from Malton in December 1958.

The 120 'Q6' 0-8-0s were the principal heavy freight engines of the North Eastern Railway, and up to the end of NER steam in 1967, No. 63363 trudges through Durham in 1959 with a southbound freight headed by five bogie bolsters loaded with large steel pipes. It was allocated to Blaydon from September 1953 until the end of 1962 when it moved to Tyne Dock. The 30 mph speed restriction sign hanging from the gantry over the line which the 'Q6' will pass is unusual.

CHAPTER 3 - NORTHWARDS FROM DARLINGTON

Relegated to freight work as early as April 1957, 'A1' Pacific No. 60158 *Aberdonian* passes through the station with a southbound freight.

Sunderland shed's 'G5' 0-4-4T No. 67300 waits in the bay with a Bishop Auckland train in the early 1950s. It was withdrawn at the end of 1955 having put in almost sixty years' service.

LM&SR-designed Ivatt Class '4' 2-6-0 No. 43126 heads a southbound Class 'H' freight on 26th September 1960. Built at Horwich in September 1951, it was always based on the North Eastern Region and was allocated to Sunderland at the date of this picture.

'O1' 2-8-0 No. 63874 from Tyne Dock shed heads south with another Class 'H' train made up of empty bogie bolsters and hoppers on 26th September 1960. It was built for the Great Central Railway by the North British Locomotive Company in 1919 as an 'O4' and was rebuilt as an 'O1' in June 1944 with a 100A boiler, Walschaerts valve gear and new cylinders.

'V3' 2-6-2T No. 67687 on a parcels train at Durham on 26th September 1960. It is buffered up to a GWR Siphon 'J', the vertically planked type which was not common. No. 67687 was allocated to Gateshead from 1957 until 2nd December 1962 when it moved to Haymarket, only to be withdrawn on the 29th. This may have been a paper-only allocation as it entered Darlington Works for cutting-up in April 1963.

'V2' 2-6-2 No. 60876 waits with a southbound express on 14th January 1961. It was built as L&NER No. 4847 in 1940 and ended its days at York, from November 1958 until withdrawn in October 1965.

Gresley 'A3' 4-6-2 No. 60081 *Shotover* from Leeds Neville Hill heads 'The North Briton' on the Up through line on 14th January 1961. It was fitted with a double chimney in October 1958 and was withdrawn four years later after covering just short of two million miles in service. 'The North Briton' ran between Glasgow/Edinburgh and Leeds until 1968.

BR Sulzer Type '2' No. D5098 on a Class '4' freight was built at Darlington in May 1960 and went new to Gateshead where it stayed until March 1963 when it was transferred to York. Renumbered to No. 24098 in February 1974, it was withdrawn in August 1975 after just fifteen years in service.

CHAPTER 3 - NORTHWARDS FROM DARLINGTON

Waiting with a Newcastle service in what was then Platform 4, Driving Motor Brake Second No. E50230 at the head of a four-car set with two two-car sets at the rear. This 1957-built Metropolitan-Cammell unit was originally used in the Hull area but was one of many re-allocated to South Gosforth where they were used primarily on services from Newcastle to Carlisle via Hexham, and to South Shields after that route was de-electrified.

The 4,000bhp single-engined Brush prototype No. HS4000 *Kestrel* approaching Durham with the 16.45 Newcastle-King's Cross in late 1969. Its days on passenger work were numbered and within a few weeks British Rail imposed a 75mph speed restriction on it for the East Coast main line, and so *Kestrel* returned to freight work. British Rail were not interested in pursuing the concept and *Kestrel* was sold in 1971 to Russia where its technology was subsequently incorporated in several Russian designs.

Durham to Sunderland

The 15 miles long Durham to Sunderland line evolved over nineteen years and was built by four different companies. The longest section, from Durham as far as Penshaw, was the 'Old Main Line' via Leamside dating back to 1844 which became a secondary route when the direct line between Penshaw and Sunderland had been in existence since 1852, primarily acting as a coal carrying railway.

Fencehouses

A Sunderland - Durham local headed by 'G5' 0-4-4T No. 67265 waits at Fencehouses in 1957. It was built for the North Eastern Railway at Darlington in 1896 as No. 1868, becoming L&NER No. 7265 in 1946. Allocated to Sunderland from 1957, this was its last year in service before withdrawal at the start of 1958 after 61 years in service. Until the advent of the big 4-4-4Ts and 4-6-2Ts, the 'G5's were the principal passenger tank engines of the NER with 110 built between 1894 and 1901. Work is well advanced on a new-build project in the North East to re-create a 'G5' for use on preserved lines. In 1949 there were fifteen Up and seventeen Down trains over the Durham to Sunderland Branch and even as late as 1963 there were still ten trains each way.

Wapping Bridge

Gresley 'V1' 2-6-2T No. 67637, probably working a Newcastle to Middlesbrough train, on 18th July 1959 at Wapping Bridge which was near Burnmoor at the end of the four-track section from Penshaw North and a mile north of Fencehouses. The signals are an unusual NER lattice post variety without finials. No. 67637 was a Gateshead engine at this time, having been transferred from Sunderland in January 1959. It would move to Heaton in June 1961 for its last year of service, entering Darlington Works for cutting on 19th February 1963.

Penshaw

On the North Eastern Region from new in January 1953, BR Standard Class '4' 4-6-0 No. 76024 at Penshaw on 27th March 1959 was allocated to West Auckland, moving to Gateshead in June 1959. Although used mainly on freight work for most of its time at West Auckland No. 76024 was possibly working a Sunderland to Durham train as this class were occasionally diagrammed for this service.

'J27' 0-6-0 No. 65892 trudges through Penshaw with a coal train in May 1963. It was one of the superheated batch of the class ordered during Raven's tenure as North Eastern Railway CME although it did not enter service until after the Grouping, in September 1923. No. 65892 was allocated to Sunderland from June 1956 until February 1964 when it went to Thornaby. Note the electricity power lines with their safety frames in case of fracture.

The BR Sulzer Type '2' was the successor to the 'J27' in the North East. No. D5105 passes Penshaw North signal box with a long train of coal empties off the Washington line in around 1966. It was completed at Darlington in September 1960 and was allocated to Gateshead until May 1974, when as No. 24105 it moved to Eastfield. It only worked in Scotland for a short time because it was stored in August 1975 and withdrawn the following October. No. D5105 was one of the class modified with high level air pipes and water tank removed for use on the Tyne Dock-Consett ore trains. The train will terminate in the extensive sidings here for onward movement by NCB locomotives to the various collieries in the vicinity.

CHAPTER 3 - NORTHWARDS FROM DARLINGTON

The centre cab, twin-engined Clayton Type '1' was billed in 1964 as the new BR standard Type '1' replacing the single-ended English Electric design. Costing over £57,000 each, they were an unmitigated disaster, breaking down within days of entering service with engine problems, and new locomotives were even put into store as they were delivered to BR to await rectification by their manufacturer. The North Eastern Region had a small batch, Nos. D8588-D8603, for local pick-up freight work and they stayed on the Region until 1970/71 when several were withdrawn, and the remainder transferred to the Scottish Region. No. D8598 which had been allocated to Gateshead from new in August 1964 was working a short Class '8' train at Penshaw North on 20th September 1966. It was transferred to Haymarket in May 1971 and withdrawn in October of that year.

4 – North Yorkshire and Durham branches and secondary lines

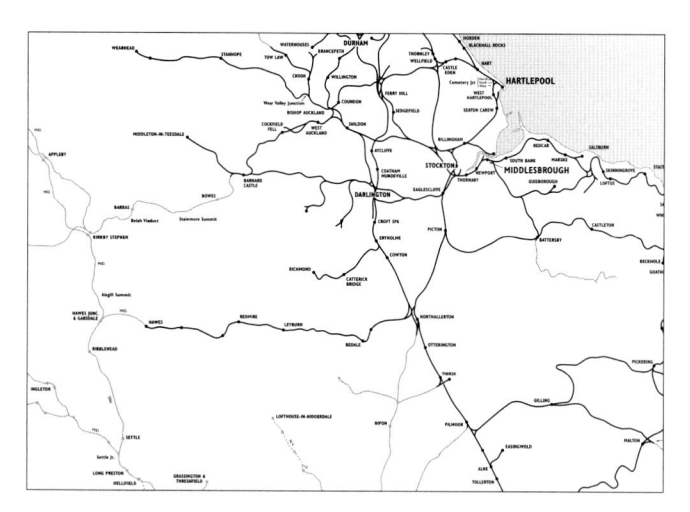

The area south of Darlington was predominantly rural without mineral deposits and therefore only a few branch lines were built, most to the west of the East Coast main line. The first one going north was the tiny Easingwold Railway which managed to remain independent throughout its existence. In contrast, were the lines to Hawes and Kirkby Stephen which met the Midland Railway's Settle & Carlisle line. From Barnard Castle, on the line which went over Stainmore Summit, there was a branch off to Middleton-in-Teesdale and, going north, a line up to West and Bishop Auckland and on to Crook and Tow Law with the Wearhead line branching off shortly after leaving Bishop Auckland. The only other branch directly off the East Coast main line went to the market town of Richmond, on the way serving the army garrison at Catterick.

The Easingwold Railway

The Easingwold Railway from Alne to Easingwold was 2½ miles long and operated under Light Railway Orders for 1896, 1912 and 1921, granted retrospectively. It opened in 1891 and remained independent until closure in 1957 despite the 1923 Grouping and nationalisation in 1948. Although it had its own locomotive for many years, latterly a standard Hudswell, Clarke 0-6-0ST from 1903, this was condemned in 1947 and the company hired in a 'J71' or 'J72' from the L&NER and then British Railways. Passenger services were withdrawn in November 1948 and goods services ceased in December 1957; the company then went into voluntary liquidation.

Right: Worsdell 'J71' 0-6-0T No. 68253 setting off from Alne with a freight to Easingwold on 19th March 1956. It was built as NER No. 239 in 1890 and was renumbered as No. 8253 in 1946. There were two freight trains on the line each day during the 1950s.

No. 68253 after arrival at Easingwold also on 19th March 1956. It was one of six 'J71' and three 'J72' 0-6-0Ts known to have worked on the line. The buffer stop marking the end of the line is on the extreme left and in the background beyond the fence is the Station Hotel built in 1892 which survives today as a private residence. Easingwold had four sidings, a passing loop and an engine shed, which was unfortunately too small to accommodate a 'J71' or 'J72'.

CHAPTER 4 - NORTH YORKSHIRE AND DURHAM BRANCHES AND SECONDARY LINES

These two pictures were taken at Easingwold on 23rd June 1957 on the occasion of the visit by the RCTS 'Yorkshire Coast Rail Tour'. The tour left Leeds City at 10.15am and diverted to Easingwold on its way to Bridlington, Scarborough and Whitby, returning to Leeds at 9.30pm.

The accommodation for the tour party consisted of ten open wagons and a brake van inscribed 'On loan to the Easingwold Light Railway'. Ten minutes were allowed for the 2½ miles from Alne and fortunately the June weather was good. The 'J71', No. 68246, had been one of the engines hired in by the railway.

The Wensleydale Branch - Northallerton to Hawes

The Wensleydale Branch from Northallerton to Hawes had been opened piecemeal over almost thirty years from 1848 with the final section from Leyburn to Hawes not completed until 1877. Apart from one double-track section between Leeming and Bedale, the line was single throughout. At Hawes, there was a joint station with the Midland Railway's branch from Hawes Junction & Garsdale on the Settle & Carlisle line.

Bedale

'B16/2' No. 61435 at Bedale on its way to Hawes with the RCTS 'North Yorkshireman' railtour on 25th April 1964. It was a rebuild in June 1937 of a Raven NER 'B16/1' 4-6-0 and was withdrawn in July 1964. No. 61435 had worked the train from Leeds City to Harrogate where it handed over to Stanier Class '5' No. 44790 which took the tour to Boroughbridge and then No. 61435 resumed at Starbeck. This was the last train to run the whole length of the Wensleydale line; the line between Redmire and Hawes was closed two days later.

Leyburn

Class 'Y3' Sentinel 0-4-0T No. 68182 at Leyburn in 1954. From 1936 until passenger services ended in April of that year, one of these shunters, No. 68159, was allocated to Northallerton and sub-shedded at Leyburn to shunt milk tanks from the dairy there. When No. 68159 was away for works attention, Darlington provided a substitute, usually No. 68182.

'J21' 0-6-0 No. 65038 at Leyburn on 25th April 1954 with a laurel wreath on its upper lamp iron as it worked the 4.10pm from Northallerton to Garsdale on the final day of passenger services to Hawes; the former Midland Railway section from Hawes to Garsdale remained open until March 1959. The 1889-built No. 65038 had been transferred to Northallerton from Newport in May 1952, but only survived the end of the Wensleydale Branch service by six months.

CHAPTER 4 - NORTH YORKSHIRE AND DURHAM BRANCHES AND SECONDARY LINES

'A8' 4-6-2T No. 69855 and 'D20' 4-4-0 No. 62360 pause at Leyburn with the Stephenson Locomotive Society and Manchester Locomotive Society 'Northern Dales Rail Tour' on 4th September 1955. They took the train from Northallerton to Hawes where No. 69855 came off and was replaced by LMR Compound 4-4-0 No. 41102. The main station building at Leyburn was situated on the goods loading platform and was joined to the goods shed.

English Electric Type '3' No. D6769 with brake tender, at the head of a westbound Class '8' freight of 25½ ton empty iron ore hoppers in use for limestone traffic for the quarry at Redmire, runs through Leyburn in the mid-1960s. It was built at Robert Stephenson & Hawthorn Ltd in July 1962 and was allocated to Thornaby until May 1992 when it was transferred to Cardiff Canton. No. D6769 was renumbered as No. 37069 under TOPS and carried the name *Thornaby TMD* from 1986 until 1992.

Hawes

'D20' 4-4-0 No. 62347 at Hawes after arrival from Northallerton in around 1953. This was originally a joint North Eastern Railway/Midland Railway station as evidenced by the architecture of the station buildings and the MR-style diagonal fencing; despite this it was always staffed by NER (later L&NER) men. The passenger service on the line was worked from the late 1930s by 'G5' 0-4-4Ts allocated to Northallerton but after nationalisation six 'D20' 4-4-0s were transferred there, including No. 62347 in March 1950, and they took over most of the passenger trains.

No. 62347 worked the final train from Northallerton to Garsdale on 25th April 1954. This turned out to not be the last passenger service on the branch because when the severe winters of 1962 and 1963 blocked the roads in Wensleydale, an emergency service was put on at the request of the local Aysgarth Rural District Council until the roads could be re-opened.

Richmond

Thompson 'L1' 2-6-4T No.67750 arrives at Richmond from Darlington on 4th August 1957. No. 67750 was built by the North British Locomotive Company at the end of 1948 and was allocated to Darlington until 1961. The 9 miles 62 chain long branch from Eryholme was opened in 1846. Traffic on the line increased substantially after Catterick Garrison was opened in 1916. However, by the 1950s the military traffic declined, although an intensive passenger service of twelve trains each way daily continued into the 1960s with DMU operation from Autumn 1957. Goods traffic ceased in 1967 and the branch was closed in March 1969 although the train shed and station building survive today, fully restored as a multi-use facility under the Richmondshire Building Preservation Trust. In the right background is the tower of Richmond Castle, described by English Heritage as the best-preserved example of an early Norman castle in England.

Bishop Auckland to Crook and Tow Law

There were through trains from Darlington to Tyneside via Bishop Auckland, Crook, Tow Law, Burnhill and along the Derwent Valley Line through Blackhill and Swalwell in North Eastern Railway days. However, increasing competition from roads and declining freight traffic resulted in the closure of the line north of Tow Law to passengers in May 1939, ending the through running to Tyneside. The service to Tow Law was cut back to Crook on 11th June 1956 and the final section from Bishop Auckland to Crook was closed to passengers on 8th March 1965.

Bishop Auckland

'A5' 4-6-2T No. 69833 at Bishop Auckland in the Crook platform during the 1950s. It was allocated to Darlington from 1939 until withdrawn in May 1957 apart from a month at Stratford in 1951. No. 69833 was one of the class built by Hawthorn, Leslie in 1925 with reduced boiler mountings and other detail differences from the original Great Central Railway design.

Fowler 2-6-4T No. 42405 passes Bishop Auckland East signal box as it arrives from Darlington, probably on a Crook train, in around 1963. It entered service nearly two years into Stanier's tenure as LM&SR Chief Mechanical Engineer and was one of the final thirty of the class built with the 'limousine' side window cab used on all of the subsequent Stanier and Fairburn 2-6-4Ts. No. 42405 was allocated to Darlington for its last three years in service, from November 1962 to October 1965.

CHAPTER 4 - NORTH YORKSHIRE AND DURHAM BRANCHES AND SECONDARY LINES

DMUs took over the Darlington to Crook service in 1957 although some trains remained steam-hauled as illustrated on the previous page. The Metropolitan-Cammell set passing Bishop Auckland East with a Darlington to Crook service had AEC 150hp engines and became Class '101' under TOPS. It was probably one of the vehicles numbered E50211/7/24 and E56063/9/76 which were allocated to Darlington and used on Richmond and Crook branch trains and on Darlington - Middleton-in-Teesdale trains. Earlier batches for the NER were built with four marker lamps on the cab front, three lower and one on top, corresponding to the lamp codes then in use. Part-way through production it was decided to introduce a two-character train describer, positioned below the centre cab window of the driving cars. This resulted in the two centre marker lights being dispensed with although the two lower outer marker lights were retained. This modification took place from Order '2f' commencing with vehicles Nos. E50210/E56062 delivered in May 1957. However, when the change was introduced in production already had the cut-outs in the cab front for the four lamps. While the two-character box covered the lower cut-out, the top one was simply plated over in a crude manner as shown in this photograph.

Crook

In 1955 there were fourteen passenger trains every weekday from Darlington to Bishop Auckland, Crook and Tow Law. 'A8' 4-6-2T No. 69872 on one of these trains waits at Crook in the mid-1950s. It was rebuilt from a North Eastern Railway 'H1' 4-4-4T in 1934 and was allocated to West Auckland from February 1949 until September 1957.

'A8' 4-6-2T No. 69851 at Crook on a service from Tow Law to Bishop Auckland and Darlington in November 1955. It was at West Auckland from May 1950 until withdrawn in November 1958. Note the 'cage' type bunker which replaced the original bunker which had conventional coal rails.

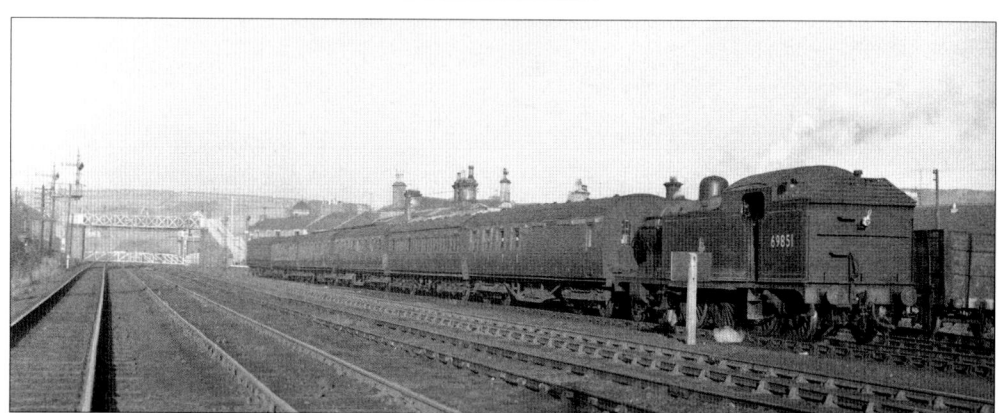

'L1' 2-6-4Ts from Darlington worked the Tow Law services alongside the West Auckland 'A8' 4-6-2Ts. No. 67680 and a Stanier Class '5' 4-6-0 were running round at Crook having brought in a football special from Derby. The 'Rams' beat non-league Crook Town 4-0 in an FA Cup First Round tie on 19th November 1955.

CHAPTER 4 - NORTH YORKSHIRE AND DURHAM BRANCHES AND SECONDARY LINES

Only two enthusiasts watch Fowler 2-6-4T No. 42405 as it moves away from the train it has brought in to Crook. Near the end of steam on the North Eastern Region, a number of ex-LM&SR tank engines were transferred to the north east to take over from former L&NER locomotives which had been withdrawn. Several Stanier engines arrived in the early 1960s together with No. 42405 and were used on the remaining local services, such as that to Crook, which had not yet been dieselised. No. 42405 had been fitted with AWS at Derby in November 1960 while it was allocated to Sowerby Bridge. It was transferred to Darlington in November 1962 and was withdrawn in October 1965. Crook station was closed to passengers in March 1965 when the service from Bishop Auckland was withdrawn.

Tow Law

'A8' 4-6-2T No. 69851 at Tow Law on a train from Darlington in November 1955. No. 69851 was rebuilt at Darlington Works in 1935 from NER 'H1' 4-4-T No. 2144 and renumbered to No. 9851 in 1946. It was at Blaydon from January 1939 until May 1950, moving to West Auckland until withdrawn in November 1958. The main station building at Tow Law was on the Down side, just visible on the extreme right. It was built in a Gothic style in local sandstone with a steeply pitched slate roof. After the passenger service north from Tow Law to Blackhill was withdrawn in May 1939, the line was closed completely from a point two miles north of the station, Tow Law becoming the terminus for trains from Darlington. Passenger numbers declined rapidly after the war and by 1951 there were just five weekday trains between Tow Law and Crook. The unprofitable Tow Law service was eventually cut back to Crook on 11th June 1956, and the station closed although goods traffic to Tow Law yard continued until 1965 when the whole line north of Wear Valley Junction was closed.

CHAPTER 4 - NORTH YORKSHIRE AND DURHAM BRANCHES AND SECONDARY LINES

BR Standard Class '3' 2-6-0 No. 77003 piloting a 4-6-2T at Tow Law, probably on the same day in November 1955 as on the previous page. It entered traffic from Swindon Works the previous year and moved to West Auckland from Darlington in July 1954 along with Nos. 77000-77002 when the class was cleared to work over the Stainmore route to Tebay. The signal box at the west end of the Up platform controlled access to the goods yard. It was similar to others in the NER's Stockton & Darlington (or Central) Division built between the 1870s and 1890s and is notable for the distinctive decorative supporting braces between the bargeboards.

Bishop Auckland to Barnard Castle

West Auckland shed

The 0-8-0s working through from Tyne Dock etc. with coke destined for Kirkby Stephen and Tebay were changed at West Auckland – for engines with a lighter axle load – at St. Helen's Colliery Sidings where the engine shed at West Auckland was situated on the north side of line towards Bishop Auckland; the shed was closed on 1st February 1964. It had been closed by the L&NER in 1931 but was re-opened four years later when Shildon shed was closed.

'J71' 0-6-0T No. 8249 at West Auckland shed was withdrawn from there in January 1953 without carrying a BR number. It has the 'E' prefix and BRITISH RAILWAYS lettering on the side tanks which date from the first few months of 1948 before the '60000' renumbering began.

A brace of 'J71' 0-6-0Ts on West Auckland shed in 1958 with No. 68269 nearest the camera and No. 68235 behind. The former had been at West Auckland since before nationalisation and stayed until withdrawn in October 1960, whereas No. 68235 did not arrive until May 1958; it was withdrawn a month after No. 68269.

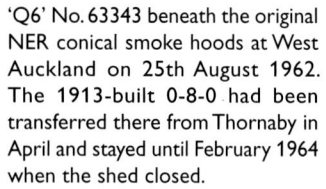

'Q6' No. 63343 beneath the original NER conical smoke hoods at West Auckland on 25th August 1962. The 1913-built 0-8-0 had been transferred there from Thornaby in April and stayed until February 1964 when the shed closed.

West Auckland

'A8' 4-6-2T No. 69875 at West Auckland with a Bishop Auckland to Barnard Castle or Middleton-in-Teesdale train in April 1957. No. 69875 was built by the NER in 1920 as a Class 'H1' 4-4-4T and was rebuilt as a 4-6-2T at Darlington during a works visit from June 1932 until January 1933. The NER Raven design had been introduced in 1913 for fast short-distance passenger work, principally on the Darlington to Saltburn service. In 1931 the L&NER rebuilt one of the class as a 4-6-2T along the lines of the GCR 'A5' 4-6-2Ts which they had multiplied after the 1923 Grouping and the other forty-four engines were rebuilt over the following five years. No. 69875 has the later Type '63B' boiler which had thinner cladding than the earlier '63A' which was flush with the smokebox. It had been transferred together with No. 69872 from Saltburn to West Auckland in early 1949. West Auckland station was closed in June 1962 when the Barnard Castle to Bishop Auckland passenger service was withdrawn.

Gresley 'V3' 2-6-2T No. 67620 at West Auckland with the SLS-RCTS 'North Eastern' railtour on 30th September 1963. This was a mammoth tour which lasted from 27th September until 1st October. On 30th September it started with No. 67620 from Newcastle and went via Leamside and Washington to Durham before continuing south to West Auckland via Crook and Tow Law. It handed over there to Fowler 2-6-4T No. 42405 which took the party on to Middleton-in-Teesdale and then Ivatt 2-6-0 No. 43129 completed the day to Whitby via Guisborough, Battersby and Grosmont. No. 67620 was built in 1931 as a 'V1' and became a 'V3' in 1953 when fitted with a higher pressure boiler; it was allocated to Gateshead from June 1963 until withdrawal in November 1964.

Cockfield Fell

'A8' 4-6-2T No. 69875 at Cockfield Fell on a train from Bishop Auckland in April 1957. The station was originally titled plain 'Cockfield' but was renamed in 1923, presumably to avoid confusion with Cockfield on the Long Melford-Bury St Edmunds Branch, which was itself renamed in 1927 as Cockfield Suffolk.

Barnard Castle

Barnard Castle was on the line from Darlington to Tebay and Penrith over Stainmore summit. It became a junction when the North Eastern Railway opened the branch to Middleton-in-Teesdale.

Two trains at the west end of Barnard Castle on 12th August 1953. On the left, Worsdell 'J21' 0-6-0 No. 65068 heads a Darlington-Kirkby Stephen-Penrith train; on the right is 'A8' 4-6-2T No. 69851 working a Sunderland to Middleton-in-Teesdale train. No. 65068 was built by the NER in 1890 as No. 300 and had been allocated to Darlington since 1949; it was withdrawn in June 1954. No. 69851 was rebuilt in 1935 from a NER 'H1' 4-4-T and was at West Auckland from May 1950 until withdrawn in November 1958.
Walter Dendy / B.W. Brooksbank collection

A decade later, little had changed at Barnard Castle except for the introduction of diesel multiple units. A Metropolitan-Cammell set waits with a Middleton-in-Teesdale service. The station was closed to passengers on 30th November 1964 after the Darlington to Middleton service was withdrawn and to goods on 6th April 1965, following closure of the Middleton line.

One of the L&NER built 'A5' 4-6-2Ts, No. 69834, takes on water at Barnard Castle while working a Bishop Auckland to Middleton train. It was built by Hawthorn, Leslie in November 1925 with reduced boiler mountings, side window cab and other detail differences from the original Great Central Railway Robinson design. The picture was taken while No. 69834 was allocated to Darlington, from October 1955 until October 1957; DMUs had taken over the service from 16th September. The three water cranes are all slightly different designs, the two on the left are definitely of NER pattern but the one on the right may just be an early L&NER design. As usual 21-ton hoppers for coal or coke traffic are stored in the holding sidings. Also note the privet bushes clipped into balls, a feature of several NER stations, notably on the approaches to York.

CHAPTER 4 - NORTH YORKSHIRE AND DURHAM BRANCHES AND SECONDARY LINES

Two different types of DMU at Barnard Castle in the summer of 1961 with, on the right, the usual Metro-Cammell variety which was the most common design in use on the NER at this time. On the left, working to Penrith over the Stainmore line, is a Birmingham Railway Carriage & Wagon Company unit, later Class '110'. Thirty sets of these, equipped with Rolls-Royce engines, were introduced from June 1961 primarily for the Calder Valley route services between Manchester and Leeds. However, the very first batch of six units went initially to Darlington, leaving to join the other class members allocated to Bradford Hammerton Street, in December 1961.

BR Standard Class '4' 2-6-0 No. 76049 pilots an LM&SR Ivatt Class '4' 2-6-0 on a Penrith-Darlington service which has come over the Stainmore line. The BR version displaced the Ivatt type on the line from May 1956 working both freight and passenger trains. No. 76049 was allocated to West Auckland from June 1956 until October 1963 when it was transferred to Hawick. Note the NER Wilkinson Trespass sign in the foreground.

BR Standard Class '3' 2-6-0 No. 77003 takes on water at Barnard Castle on 20th January 1962, the last day of the Stainmore line to Kirkby Stephen and Penrith. It was working the RCTS 'Stainmore Limited' from Darlington together with Class '4' 2-6-0 No. 76049 and is adorned with a wreath on the smokebox door. For some unknown reason, the two headlamps have been taken from the lower lamp irons and placed together on the upper iron.

Middleton-in-Teesdale

Although Middleton-in-Teesdale was in County Durham, the station itself was in Yorkshire with the county boundary formed by the River Tees a short distance to the north of the station. It was the terminus of the 8¾ miles long branch from Barnard Castle which opened on 13th May 1868 and until 1894 the station was just plain 'Middleton'.

'G5' 0-4-4T No. 67305 at Middleton-in-Teesdale after arrival with the push-pull from Darlington in September 1957. In the mid-1950s there were three return trips from Middleton to Darlington. The first arrival there was at 7.28am and since the next departure was not until 12.39pm the set worked to Richmond as the 7.55am and the 8.42am back to Darlington. No. 67305 was built in 1897 at Darlington Works as NER No. 1755 and was fitted with push-pull apparatus in 1941. It became L&NER No. 7305 in November 1946 and was withdrawn at the end of 1958 after spending its final year at North Blyth.

Lens of Sutton Association

No. 67305 has now moved onto the run-round loop to take on water. On the left is the stone base of the original water tank from which locomotives took water directly. This was replaced in the 1890s by the larger tank on the right supported by timber pillars and with a water column alongside from which No. 67305 is being topped up. The base was then used as a platelayers' hut with a brick chimney passing through the old tank. The 'G5' 0-4-4T was one of the two regular engines, together with No. 67284, on the push-pull service at this time. The engine working the last train of the day was stabled in the Middleton sub-shed overnight and at the weekend. No. 67305 was allocated to Darlington from November 1952 until November 1957.

Lens of Sutton Association

CHAPTER 4 - NORTH YORKSHIRE AND DURHAM BRANCHES AND SECONDARY LINES

L&NER-built 'A5' 4-6-2T No. 69834 after arriving at Middleton-in-Teesdale with a Bishop Auckland service in 1957. The station had a single platform with a run-round loop and the goods yard was at the rear of the platform. There was originally a 45ft turntable on the run-round line, but this was removed in the 1940s. The shed, visible on the right of this photograph, continued to be used by 'G5' 0-4-4Ts from Darlington right up until steam traction was ousted by DMUs on 16th September 1957; it was demolished in 1961. In its early days Middleton station had attractive gardens on the platform and a lily pond on the approach road and was a regular prize winner in the annual Best Kept Stations competition. However, by the 1950s the gardens were overgrown, full of stones and broken branches and thick slime clogged the pond. The wife of the newly appointed stationmaster decided to restore the gardens and with the help of the local staff, transformed the station with flower beds, rockeries, a waterfall and a fountain, some of which can be seen to the left of No. 69834.

Little had changed at Middleton-in-Teesdale since DMUs took over the service in late 1957 as illustrated by this 1963 view of a Metropolitan-Cammell two-car unit which appears to be towing a full brake. After the withdrawal of the Barnard Castle to Penrith service in January 1962, through running from Sunderland and Newcastle ceased and all Middleton trains started at Darlington with seven trains daily from Darlington to Barnard Castle, five of which continued to Middleton. The Darlington-Barnard Castle-Middleton-in-Teesdale passenger service ended on 30th November 1964, but freight lingered on for a few months, until April 1965.
R. Darlaston

Thompson 'L1' 2-6-4T No. 67646 working bunker-to-bunker with LM&SR Stanier 2-6-4T No. 42639 at Middleton-in-Teesdale with the RCTS 'North Yorkshireman' rail tour on 25th April 1964. The pair were backing the special out of the platform before taking the train back to Darlington where they handed over to 'V2' 2-6-2 No. 60855 for the final leg back to Leeds City. The L&NER running-in board had metal letters screwed to a wooden board, and after nationalisation the North Eastern Region repainted it in the regional tangerine colour. This was the limit to the updating of the platform signage since enamel totem signs were never installed there or at the other three stations on the branch.

The Wearhead Branch

The Wearhead Branch was twenty-two miles long and left the Bishop Auckland to Crook line at Wear Valley Junction. Up until the withdrawal of the passenger service in June 1953 there were four trains each way on weekdays. Goods traffic continued up the valley as far as St. John's Chapel, the station before Weardale, until 1961. A passenger service was reinstated by the Weardale Railway from Bishop Auckland to Stanhope in 2010 and currently there is a seasonal service of heritage passenger trains operated over the sixteen mile section.

The last train to Wearhead headed by North Eastern 'J21' 0-6-0 No. 65078 waits to leave Bishop Auckland at 7.47pm on 27th June 1953. *Ben Brooksbank*

The terminus at Wearhead was provided with a single road engine shed on the right of the photograph, a turntable, run-round loop and goods shed. In the station, waiting to make its last journey down Weardale on 27th June 1953 is 'J21' 0-6-0 No. 65078. *Ben Brooksbank*

A close-up view of the last train preparing to leave Wearhead for Bishop Auckland. No. 65078 was an ex-NER Worsdell Class 'C', becoming a 'J21' under the L&NER. It was built in 1891 as NER No. 1554, renumbered in 1946 as No. 5078, and withdrawn as BR 65078 in February 1957. *Ben Brooksbank*

5 – Sunderland to Hartlepool

Sunderland station

Sunderland Central station opened in 1879 when the NER concentrated the traffic from its three existing termini into a new centrally-located station. The site was, however, constricted with a tunnel at the north end and retaining walls on both sides. A 95ft-span arched roof covered two narrow island platforms and all the passenger facilities had to be carried above the tracks on arches. During the Second World War the central section of the train shed was damaged in an air raid and it was replaced by glass and steel verandas; the remainder of the train shed was removed in 1953 and the verandas extended.

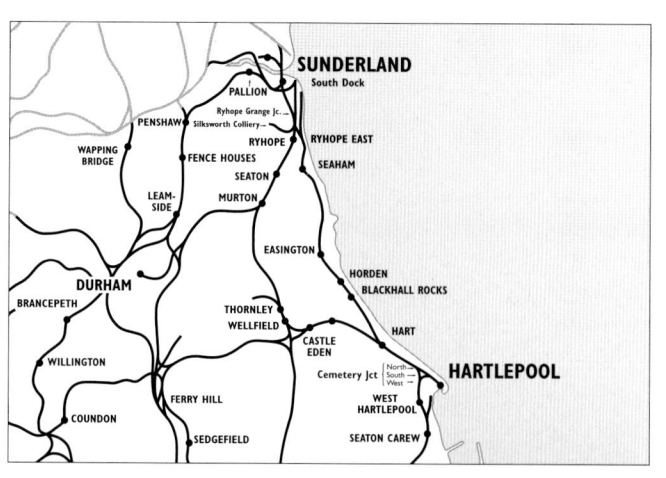

'G5' 0-4-4T No. 67263 arrives at Sunderland on 30th April 1952 showing the remains of the arched roof and the short 1944 verandas. No. 67263 was allocated to Durham until 1956 when it moved to South Blyth. The gloom of the post-war Sunderland Central station is relieved only by the large sign for Binns Department store. This was often described as the 'Harrods of the north', and the business developed rapidly in the second half of the nineteenth century with the flagship Sunderland store increasing in size even right up to the 1960s. New shops were opened in the 1920s in the north of England and Scotland, and the advertising slogan 'Shop at Binns' was created in 1924; this was to adorn the front of the Sunderland Corporation buses and trams for the next fifty years. The company was taken over by House of Fraser in 1953; it contracted during the final decades of the twentieth century before closure in January 1993.

H.C. Casserley

'G5' 0-4-4T No. 67254 in Platform 2 at Sunderland with a local service to Durham in 1956. In the early 1950s there were fifteen Up and seventeen Down trains each day over the branch to Durham via Penshaw and Fencehouses. No. 67254 was allocated to Sunderland shed from October 1955 until withdrawn at the end of 1957. The arched roof shown in the picture above has now gone and the verandas extended.

'V3' 2-6-2T No. 67682 waits at Sunderland's Platform 4, probably working a Newcastle service, on 3rd October 1954. It was at Gateshead from October 1950 until the end of 1954 when it went to Hexham. The local trains between Newcastle and Sunderland remained steam-hauled until August 1958 although DMUs had taken over the Newcastle to Middlesbrough service in November 1955. For some unknown reason, the station did not have the standard BR totem signs but instead the electric lights hung from the verandas had brick-shaped diffusers inscribed with the name 'Sunderland' – without the Central suffix.

The man nearest the camera looks up from his book as the now-preserved 'J27' 0-6-0 No. 65894 trundles through with a Class '8' freight in 1967. It was the last of the class to enter service, out-shopped from Darlington North Road Works in September 1923 as No. 2392. They were the largest North Eastern Railway 0-6-0s and were originally classed as 'P3' until 1926. A total of 115 were built between 1906 and 1923, fifty from external builders, and the final thirty-five were fitted with superheaters and piston valves, although many including No. 65894 received non-superheated boilers from 1943 onwards. No. 65894 spent most of its post-nationalisation career at York, until October 1966 when it was transferred to Sunderland South Dock. On 9th September 1967 it worked the last diagrammed steam turn from the shed and was purchased directly from British Railways by the North Eastern Locomotive Preservation Group in December 1967. After restoration to full working order, it went to the North Yorkshire Moors Railway in October 1971 and has spent much of its post-BR working life there. It has had several major overhauls during this time, the last of which was completed in late 2018.
John Atkinson

The sign indicates that the passengers on Platform 3 at Sunderland are about to board the Metropolitan-Cammell DMU on an 'All Stations to Newcastle – except Monkwearmouth' on 8th June 1963. The Birmingham Railway Carriage & Wagon Company two-car DMU, later Class '104', on the left had arrived on a service from South Shields; DMUs had taken over this service in August 1958 and it lasted until June 1965. These units had worksplates which omitted the more familiar 'Railway' from the builder's name.

Another Birmingham Railway Carriage & Wagon Company DMU which, according to the 'B4' headcode, was working a Newcastle-Sunderland service, at the south end of Sunderland station on 3rd June 1964. As this picture clearly shows, the station was in the middle of an extensive modernisation programme. The distinctive 118ft-high French Gothic style clock tower is still in place but would soon be demolished. The work was completed in November 1965 with a concrete deck, supporting over twenty retail outlets, covering all of the platforms replacing the steel awnings; the two island platforms were retained.

CHAPTER 5 - SUNDERLAND TO HARTLEPOOL

South from Sunderland

'V2' 2-6-2 No. 60846 departs southwards from Sunderland Central with a parcels train and is about to enter the tunnel below Mowbray Park heading towards Ryhope Grange Junction on 1st April 1959. The line on the left of the cabins is from Penshaw via Pallion. The sign for Binns Department Store is partially visible in the top right of the picture; the company had shops on either side of Fawcett Street alongside the station for many years.

On a cold winter's day in 1966, 'Q6' 0-8-0 No. 63346 has passed under Holmeside bridge and is approaching the station platform with a northbound freight. It had been built in March 1913 as NER No. 1253 and became No. 3346 under the L&NER 1946 renumbering scheme. No. 63346 had been transferred from Consett to Sunderland in October 1964.

Villette Road

BR Sulzer Type '4' No. D166 passes Villette Road signal box on 26th June 1962. The 'Peak' went new to Gateshead on 9th May and was there for six years before transferring to Holbeck; it became No. 46029 under TOPS and was withdrawn in January 1983. The last coach of the train has just emerged from the tunnel under Mowbray Park. The large building in the right background is the Toward Road bus depot of United Automobile Services which had been 50% owned by the L&NER since 1929; it was nationalised in 1948 and became part of the National Bus Company in 1969.

In the early days of the 'Big Freeze' of 1963 English Electric Type '4' No. D243 heads a southbound express past Villette Road signal box on 16th January. Built in 1959, it was at Gateshead until January 1966 and was withdrawn ten years later, as No. 40043. By the date of this picture the coaches stabled in the carriage sidings were used only for summer excursions.

Grangetown

English Electric Type '4' No. D354 had been in traffic for only a month when photographed with an Up express at Grangetown, two miles out of Sunderland, on 22nd August 1961. The picture was taken looking north from Spelter Works Road bridge.

Five years later, the scene has not changed as 'J27' 0-6-0 No. 65873 takes a loaded coal train on 21st September 1966. The 1922-built engine was withdrawn from Sunderland shed the following month.

The last summer for this timeless scene, as 'J27' No. 65892 heads a train of empties towards Sunderland in 1967 through Grangetown. It had been transferred from North Blyth in October 1966 to Sunderland and was withdrawn in August 1967.

English Electric Type '4' No. D387 approaching Ryhope Grange Junction on 16th June 1962. It had only entered service on 11th April as evidenced by the paint still on the buffer heads. No. D387 was working a heavy parcels train carrying traffic from the Littlewoods mail order catalogue call centre at Commercial Road in the Hendon district of Sunderland. This was opened in 1955 under the name Brian Mills and increased with the Burlington brand in 1958; the centre closed in 2010.

Sunderland South Dock shed

Sunderland South Dock was coded 54A by British Railways but changed to 52G on 15th September 1958 when the Sunderland Motive Power District was incorporated within the Gateshead District. During the 1950s, the shed had an allocation covering both passenger and freight working, with around twenty 0-6-0s for the latter and the former handled by a dozen or more 'G5' 0-4-4Ts plus a smaller number of 'A8' 4-6-2Ts; shunting was covered by a mix of NER 0-6-0Ts and 'J94' 0-6-0STs. There was an influx of more modern 'J39' 0-6-0s between 1959 and 1961, but they were soon withdrawn and the elderly 'J27's carried on until 1967; the main roundhouse was closed in September of that year when steam traction was finally eliminated from the area but the smaller straight shed remained open for diesel stabling and minor maintenance.

'A8' 4-6-2T No. 69853 at its home shed in 1958, still with a 54A shedplate. It had been rebuilt from 'H1' 4-4-4T No. 2146 in 1935 and has a modified 'cage' type bunker and a later Type '63B' boiler. No. 69853 had been at Sunderland since May 1948 and was withdrawn from there in January 1960 along with No. 69855. Sunderland had several of these big tanks in the early 1950s. Seven more arrived in September 1957, mainly displaced from Saltburn and Middlesbrough by DMUs, followed by four more in 1958; all had been withdrawn by mid-1960.

Worsdell 'J25' 0-6-0 No. 65666 outside the shed on 17th May 1959. One of four of the class on Sunderland's books in the late 1950s, it had been transferred from Tyne Dock a year earlier and lasted for another year before being withdrawn in July 1960. Note the locomotive headlamp left hanging from the post.

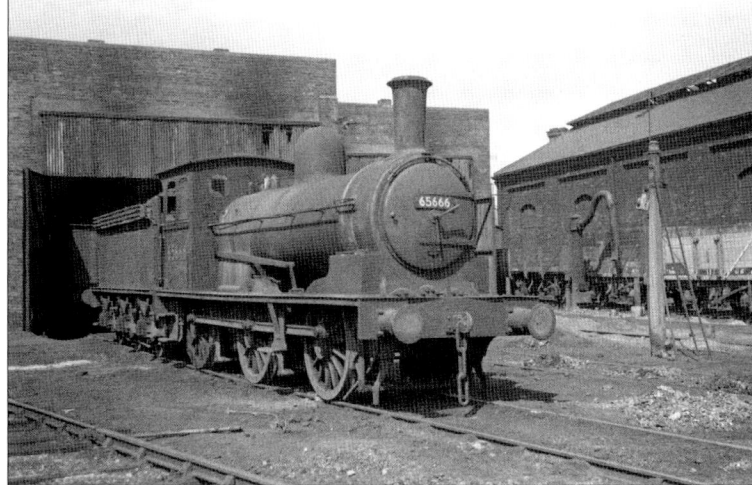

Although Sunderland had five 'J39' 0-6-0s during the early 1950s, three of these left in June 1956. However, ten more arrived in late 1959, followed by a further dozen over the next two years. Three of these were on shed on 25 August 1962, Nos. 64851, 64847 and 64701, but all had gone by the end of the year. Only two were transferred away and the remainder, including the three pictured, were withdrawn.

Two 'J27' 0-6-0s inside the shed on 21st August 1967, Sunderland's No. 65855 with a hand-painted 52G shed code and No. 65811 which had been transferred from Blyth in May but still carried the 52F shedplate. Both engines had been in service for over fifty-nine years. No. 65811 was built by the North British Locomotive Company three months before No. 65855 was built by Beyer, Peacock in August 1908.

Sunderland Shed near the end, in 1967. By the time of this picture, the passenger tanks had long gone and there were no 0-6-0Ts on the books. With 'K1' 2-6-0 No. 62012 which had been transferred from York in April but was withdrawn within a month, 'Q6' 0-8-0 No. 63458 went in July and 'J27' No. 65892 in August. The final steam workings from the shed were on the Silksworth Colliery Branch, the Monkwearmouth-Hilton Colliery Branch and coal from Seaham to either Tees Yard or the Tyneside power stations. The small straight shed which was later used for diesel stabling is on the extreme left.

John Atkinson

English Electric Type '3' diesels took over freight work from the NER 'J27' and 'Q6' classes but they often needed brake tenders to provide sufficient braking force to work the unfitted trains still prevalent in the early 1970s. No. D6765 and a classmate sandwich a brake tender at Sunderland on 1st June 1970. It has full yellow ends and TOPS data panels but otherwise is still in green livery with serif pattern stock numbers. It went new to Thornaby in November 1962 but had been transferred to Gateshead in January 1970; it was withdrawn in 2007 as No. 37065.

Londonderry Junction

An unidentified 'Q6' 0-8-0 trudges north with a long train of empties past Londonderry Junction signal box in 1966. Despite the name which derived from the Marquis of Londonderry, this was at Hendon near Sunderland South Dock. The line was built by the Londonderry, Seaham and Sunderland Railway to connect Seaham to the docks, primarily to convey coal from the pits owned by the Londonderry family, and was taken over by the North Eastern Railway in 1900. This view is looking south down the Londonderry (Hendon) Branch towards Ryhope Grange Junction where it met the line from Sunderland Central.

Ryhope Grange Junction

'Q6' 0-8-0 No. 63346 with a brake van for its next train coming down from Hendon towards Ryhope Grange Junction on 13th May 1967. The line to Sunderland Central is just visible to the left of No. 63346, diverging under the bridge. The 'Q6' had been transferred from Consett to Sunderland in October 1964 and was withdrawn from there on 29th May 1967.

Working back with a full load for South Dock, No. 63346 takes the right fork at Ryhope Grange Junction. Note the cut back coal rails on the tender.

CHAPTER 5 - SUNDERLAND TO HARTLEPOOL

'K1' No. 62042 with northbound coal hoppers at Ryhope Grange Junction takes the line towards Sunderland Central on 13th May 1967. No. 62042 was built by the North British Locomotive Company in October 1949 and had been transferred to Sunderland from York in April 1967; it only stayed there for a month and went to West Hartlepool from where it was withdrawn a month later. The Peppercorn 2-6-0s were not well-liked in some parts of the North East because their braking when working loose-coupled heavy trains was poor compared with the home-grown 0-6-0s and 0-8-0s which perhaps explains its short stay at Sunderland. Ryhope Grange signal box is on the right behind the train and the tracks on the left of the picture go towards Londonderry Junction.

BR Sulzer Type '2' No. D5112 with a parcels train at Ryhope Grange Junction on 26th July 1967. It had come up the coast line from Hartlepool – the tracks on the right are the former Durham and Sunderland Railway line over Seaton Bank. No. D5112 was completed at Darlington Works in December 1960 and went new to Gateshead. It then spent over three years at Thornaby before returning to Gateshead in June 1964; it was transferred to Holbeck in October 1967. It has a cast 52A shedplate on the cab front and when given a yellow warning panel lost the frame-level stripe across the cab front. No. D5112 moved to Scotland in 1971, becoming No. 24112 in 1974 and was withdrawn at the end of 1976.

Ryhope Colliery Junction and the Silksworth Colliery Branch

A short branch ran from the Durham and Sunderland Railway immediately to the south of Ryhope Grange Junction to the Ryhope and Silksworth Collieries which were both part of the Marquis of Londonderry's empire. Ryhope was opened in 1857 and closed in November 1966; Silksworth opened in 1869 and closed in November 1971.

A well-cleaned 'J27' 0-6-0, the now preserved No. 65894, and its train of empty coal hoppers at Ryhope Colliery Junction is signalled onto the branch towards Ryhope and Silksworth Collieries in summer 1967. No. 65894 spent its final months at Sunderland, moving from York in October 1966.

'J27' No. 65880 comes off the Ryhope/Silksworth Colliery Branch approaching Ryhope Colliery Junction in 1967. It was double track as far as Ryhope & Silksworth Colliery Junction, opposite Ryhope St. Paul's Church in the background, where a single line continued to each colliery. No. 65880 was built in 1922 as NER No. 2358 and was allocated to Sunderland for its last six months in service up to withdrawal in June 1967.

CHAPTER 5 - SUNDERLAND TO HARTLEPOOL

At Ryhope & Silksworth Colliery Junction in summer 1967, a very clean 'J27' No. 65882 is coming off the single-track branch from Silksworth Colliery with a loaded train, whilst another 0-6-0 waits to go up the branch with a train of empties. The two lines in the foreground led to Ryhope Colliery which had closed in November 1966.

The brakes will be pinned down for this load of 'fulls' from Silksworth Colliery as it runs down to the junction hauled by a 'J27' on 29th June 1967.

It is easy to see from this picture why the branch attracted the attention of photographers as steam drew to a close in the North East, especially since there were usually three trips every morning and three in the late afternoon/evening. 'J27' No. 65882 with at least twenty empty hopper wagons slogs up the three mile climb to Silksworth Colliery. It was built by the North Eastern Railway before the 1923 Grouping and entered service in August 1922. No. 65882 was one of four of the class transferred to Sunderland from North Blyth in May 1967; it was withdrawn in September when the shed closed.

There are only three loaded wagons behind No. 65882 which is taking three loaded hoppers up to the Colliery. It is likely that they contained coal of a different type than that mined at Silksworth, from another colliery, which had been ordered for sale there.

Two of what became Class '03' under TOPS, Nos. D2074 and D2094, at Silksworth Colliery in October 1969. Following the withdrawal of steam, pairs of these 204bhp shunters coupled in this formation hauled coal between the colliery and Sunderland South Dock. Unlike some, they were not a semi-coupled pair because No. D2094 was the only one fitted with air brakes. Both locomotives were built at Doncaster Works, No. D2074 in November 1959 and No. D2094 in June 1960. No. D2074 was withdrawn in May 1972 but No. D2094 lasted until 1988. It was then sold to Parkfield Castings which operated from the former BR Works at Horwich and when that firm closed down it was purchased for preservation by the South Yorkshire Railway Preservation Society at Meadowhall in Sheffield. It was subsequently purchased privately and is now based on The Royal Deeside Railway in Scotland.

The Durham and Sunderland Railway

The Durham and Sunderland Railway was opened in the first half of the nineteenth century to transport coal from the mines en route to the River Wear. It originally employed rope haulage over the middle part of the line, around nine miles between Shincliffe and Seaton including the fearsome 1 in 44 of Seaton Bank. The line ran into financial difficulties and became part of the NER in 1854. Passenger services ended in January 1953, but freight continued until 1993, clearing coal stocks after Murton Colliery closed in November 1991.

Ryhope

Viewed from the now restored preserved footbridge at the north end of Ryhope (West) station in early 1967, 'J27' No. 65811 takes empties towards Seaton. The Ford Anglia parked on the left probably belonged to the photographer. No. 65811 had been allocated to Blyth since before nationalisation but spent its final three months in traffic at Sunderland. It was built for the NER by the North British Locomotive Company in May 1908 and was numbered 1015 until February 1946 when it became No. 5811. Ryhope station closed to passengers in 1953; Ryhope East, which was to the right of the picture on the line running down the coast towards Hartlepool, remained open until 1960.

Seaton Bank

'Q6' 0-8-0 No. 63395 produces a wonderful display of smoke as it climbs Seaton Bank in summer 1967. It was built by the NER in December 1918 as Class 'T2' No. 2238 and spent its first twenty-five years at Blaydon Depot before moving during the Second World War to Newport (Middlesbrough), then later to Darlington, West Hartlepool, Hull Dairycoates, Selby and Consett. No. 63395 was transferred to Sunderland in May 1965 and was not withdrawn until steam ended there in September 1967. Following withdrawal, it was purchased by the North Eastern Locomotive Preservation Group in April 1968 and after restoration moved in 1970 to the North Yorkshire Moors Railway where it worked until 1982 and was then stored for eighteen years. After a lengthy overhaul completed in 2016, it returned to service on the Railway.

The inland route between Sunderland and Hartlepool

Thornley

A tender-first 'J27' brings a coal train off the Thornley Colliery Branch at Thornley Junction on the inland Sunderland to Hartlepool route. This picture is taken looking north with Thornley station and its typical tall NER signal box in the background. Thornley was on the line built by the Hartlepool Dock & Railway Company in the 1830s which reached as far north as Haswell, a short distance from the Durham and Sunderland railway at Murton, and the gap was filled by a chord opened by the NER in 1877, the HD&R having been swallowed up by that company in 1854.

Wellfield

When the English Electric Type '3's began to take over the coal trains from the 'Q6' 0-8-0s and the 'J27' 0-6-0s they needed brake tenders to provide sufficient braking capacity when working heavy unfitted trains. No. D6756 from Thornaby Depot passes the site of Wellfield station, which was closed in 1952, with a southbound Class '8' coal train on 14th June 1965. It was renumbered twice, as No. 37056 in 1974 and then again in 1987 as No. 37513 after it was refurbished and re-geared with CP7 bogies and fitted with a Brush BA1005A main alternator. It was sent to France for use on TGV construction work in September 1999 and returned in July 2000; it was eventually scrapped in 2008 after spending most of the time in store although it was on hire for Sandite duties. Wellfield had once been an important railway crossroad where the north-south line between Sunderland and Teesside crossed the east-west line from Hart to Ferryhill. The 1910 built signal box, formerly sited on the southbound platform, is not of the usual NER style due to the restricted width site and the need to overhang the platform. It replaced a box situated south of the station originally called 'Castle Eden North Junction', controlling the junction of the line to Bowesfield Junction where it joined the route of Stockton & Darlington Railway.

Along the coast to Hartlepool

The original Hartlepool to Sunderland inland route via Thornley, Haswell, and Murton required trains to traverse both the 1 in 52 incline northbound at Hesleden and the 1 in 44 southbound at Seaton Bank, and so at the end of the 19th century the North Eastern Railway began construction of a new, more direct route along the coast. The first northern section of this had been built in the 1850s by the Londonderry, Seaham & Sunderland Railway to take coal traffic from Seaham via Ryhope to the South Docks at Sunderland and in 1900, the NER purchased its Seaham to Sunderland line. Southwards, a new eleven miles long line was built from Seaham Colliery station to a junction with the former Hartlepool Dock & Railway line at Hart Junction. It had to cross the denes at Hawthorn, Castle Eden and Crimdon, requiring construction of three substantial viaducts. It was opened in April 1905 with new stations provided at Blackhall Rocks, Horden and Easington.

Ryhope East

A Metropolitan-Cammell diesel multiple unit on a Newcastle to Middlesbrough service at Ryhope East on 24th April 1957. The busy 7.0am departure from Newcastle required two four-car sets as illustrated here. DMUs had replaced the hourly steam service hauled by 'A8' 4-6-2Ts or 'V1' 2-6-2Ts in November 1955 using five Derby 'Lightweight' 4-car sets. These were replaced by Metropolitan-Cammell four-car units which had a stronger and heavier integral-type body from late 1956. More sets were delivered to South Gosford Depot in September and October 1957, with the displaced 'Lightweights' moving to the Newcastle-Carlisle service. The set illustrated has no speed 'whiskers' on the cab front and four steam-style marker lights. Classified as '101' under TOPS, the class was numerically the largest in British Railways' DMU fleet, totalling 637 vehicles, and many of them were refurbished from 1974 onwards.

Seaham

A Gresley 'V3' 2-6-2T arrives at Seaham station with a seven-coach southbound evening express on 6th July 1957. The station was originally named 'Seaham Colliery' and the 'Colliery' was dropped in 1925 when the original 'Seaham' station became 'Seaham Harbour'. New houses are being built opposite the Vane Tempest Colliery Welfare Institute which is the large building behind the platform shelter. Note the empty pigeon baskets all labelled up and ready for return. The station remains in use today with an hourly service in each direction.

'Q6' 0-8-0 No. 63405 brings empty hoppers from the north through Seaham on a dismal wet day in 1966. It was built as NER No. 2248 at Darlington in June 1919 and had been allocated to Sunderland since July 1963. It was withdrawn at the end of 1966, three years short of a half-century in service.

At the south end of the station No. 63405 passes over the level crossing towards the pointwork at the approach to the colliery exchange sidings which are on the right, obscured by the signal box. There is an NCB saddle tank visible to the left of the signal. Note the concrete sleepered track which appears to have been re-laid recently and that classic 1960s Hillman Imp parked by the shops on the left.

Another 'Q6', No. 63395, takes a loaded train north, probably on the same day as the pictures on the previous page. The locomotive is now preserved.

'J27' 0-6-0 No. 65892 about to pass Seaham signal box with northbound loaded hopper wagons on 24th May 1967. This picture shows more of the colliery exchange sidings on the right. Seaham Colliery was opened in 1849 by the Londonderry family and closed in 1988. Built under the L&NER in August 1923 as No. 2390, No. 65892 had been transferred to Sunderland from North Blyth in late 1966 and was in service until August 1967.

Hawthorn Dene

The viaduct over Hawthorn Dene was one of three built by the NER for the new coastal line south from Seaham. The brick-built Grade II listed viaduct is located near the coast at the mouth of Hawthorn Burn, by Hive Point, just over a mile east of Hawthorn Village.

A 'Q6' with a brake van makes its way over the viaduct in summer 1967. The line northwards closely follows the coast with Dawdon Colliery in the distance.

With the North Sea providing a perfect backdrop, 'J27' No. 65833 crosses Hawthorn Dene Viaduct with a southbound coal train. It was built for the NER by Robert Stephenson & Hawthorn in 1909 and numbered 1056. It was at Sunderland from April 1962 until withdrawn in May 1967; this picture was taken during its last year in service.

'J27' No. 65882 heads south over Hawthorn Dene Viaduct towards Easington Colliery. The picture was taken while it was allocated to Sunderland, between May 1967 and its withdrawal in September.

With Easington Colliery in the background, WD 'Austerity' 2-8-0 No. 90348 heads a southbound freight down the coast on 21st August 1967. It had been transferred to Sunderland in October 1966 after spending over eight years at Wakefield.

Denemouth (Castle Eden) Viaduct

The viaduct at Dene Holme over Castle Eden Dene was between Blackhall Colliery and Horden. It was 141 feet from the ground to rail level and had ten arches, each spanning 60ft. There was a wooden pedestrian walkway on the seaward side of the bridge which was in use up to the 1950s. The construction of the three viaducts on the coastal line required the opening of a special brickfield and, at Castle Eden, the creation of a temporary 800ft long cableway across the valley.

'K1' 2-6-0 No. 62041 with a short southbound mixed freight crosses Castle Eden Viaduct. It was at West Hartlepool from March 1966 until withdrawn in April 1967. In the distance, a DMU is in the platform at Horden station and beyond that is Horden Colliery, which was opened in 1900, primarily to extract the coal from under the sea; it closed in 1987.

On the same day as the previous picture, a view of the viaduct from below rail level as a two-car Metropolitan-Cammell DMU crosses over Castle Eden Dene. The left-hand vehicle is newly-repainted in British Rail secondary passenger colours of plain blue – a livery which was much less attractive than the lined green of the trailing vehicle.

Blackhall

'Q6' 0-8-0 No. 63345 slowly makes its way south with twenty loaded hoppers at Blackhall Rocks on 5th February 1964. It had been at Sunderland since mid-1962 but was within two months of withdrawal when photographed.

Hart

'Q6' 0-8-0 No.63456 at Hart station is coming off the coastal line from Seaham and Easington with a train of hoppers on 6th February 1964. Although the running-in board was still there, the station had closed in August 1953. The track on the left of the signal box goes to Castle Eden and then either up to Thornley and Murton, or on to Ferryhill. Note the NER bracket signal with its McKenzie & Holland finial. A more austere L&NER replacement signal complete with repeater arm on the tall post is in the centre. It has a small wooden platform for access to the lower lamp. A permanent way gang is just beyond the box waiting for the train to pass.

Cemetery Junction

Alongside the old cemetery at Hartlepool, the lines formed a triangle which gave the three junctions at its points their names. The line at the North Junction went up to Hart, the one at the South Junction to the original Hartlepool station and the Fish Dock, and the one at the West Junction to West Hartlepool.

Peppercorn 'K1' 2-6-0 No. 62041 coming from Cemetery Junction West towards Cemetery Junction South with a train made up of both 16-ton mineral wagons and 20-ton hoppers on 25th March 1967. No. 62041 was built by the North British Locomotive Company in October 1949. It had been transferred to West Hartlepool from Darlington in March 1966 and was withdrawn within three weeks of this picture.

On the same day another 'K1', No. 62044, travels in the opposite direction towards Cemetery Junction West. From there, the line went almost due south past the extensive timber yards and docks before turning east to run into West Hartlepool station. No. 62044 was also built by the North British Locomotive Company in October 1949, arrived at West Hartlepool shed at the same time as No. 62041 but was not withdrawn until the end of June. Note the badly sheeted 16-ton Iron Ore Tipplers; we are not sure what they would be carrying, since iron ore did not require protection from the elements so they must have been borrowed for other traffic.

West Hartlepool

West Hartlepool station
The first Hartlepool station was originally built as the coastal terminus of the Hartlepool Dock & Railway in 1839 but when a new through station at West Hartlepool was opened in 1880 this became the town's principal station. From then onwards until 1947, Hartlepool station became merely the terminus of a shuttle service from West Hartlepool, although it continued to handle school traffic until 1964. Following the merger of West Hartlepool with Hartlepool on 26th April 1967, the former was renamed plain Hartlepool.

'G5' 0-4-4T No. 67324 at the north end of the station waits to depart with a train to Sunderland on 11th August 1956. It had been transferred from Darlington to West Hartlepool in July 1953 but succumbed in November 1957 after the introduction of large numbers of DMUs to the North Eastern Region local services.

On the same August day, 'J27' 0-6-0 No. 65865 rounds the curve through West Hartlepool with a train of Iron Ore wagons – a hopper at the front followed by branded 16-tonners. No. 65865 was at West Hartlepool from October 1953 until February 1959 when it moved to Thornaby. From the mid-19th century, large amounts of timber were imported through the railway-owned docks at West Hartlepool for use in shipbuilding and for pit props in the mining industry and the extensive timber yards partly visible in the right background developed alongside the Timber Dock.

'A2' 4-6-2 No. 60539 *Bronzino* gets underway with a northbound express in July 1961. This could well be a diversion of a Newcastle train which was commonplace at the time. *Bronzino* was the first of the Peppercorn 'A2' Pacifics to be built with a double Kylchap exhaust following disappointing steaming of the engines built with single chimneys. It was allocated to Heaton shed from new in August 1948 until September 1961 when it was transferred to Tweedmouth along with four other Heaton 'A2's displaced by new diesels.

'A1' 4-6-2 No. 60150 Willbrook with a southbound parcels train in June 1964. A Southern Railway BY van leads the train which will be carrying Brian Mills mail order traffic from its depot in Sunderland. After spending over a decade at Gateshead, No. 60150 was transferred to York in November 1960 and was withdrawn from there in October 1964, after only fifteen years in service. Note the artistic decoration of the rivet heads on the smokebox door and the oil lamps perched on top of the electric lamps.

Ivatt Class '4' 2-6-0 No. 43100 at the east end of the station with an interesting train of cut-down NER hopper wagons carrying pit-props. These wagons were normally for internal use at the wood yard but were possibly being used for a short transfer working over BR metals. Historically, there were large numbers of wagons full of timber because the structure of the demurrage charges meant that larger merchants had free storage for periods of up to eighteen months. No. 43100 was built at Darlington in February 1951 and transferred to West Hartlepool in November 1959; it worked from there until withdrawal in February 1967.

Another Ivatt 2-6-0, No. 43128, rounds the curve at the north of the station with a train of timber conveyed in a mix of wagons; the first two are 13T wooden mineral wagons, followed by more cut-down hoppers. Built at Horwich for the North Eastern Region in October 1951, No. 43128 was a West Hartlepool engine from July 1956 until withdrawn in July 1965.

Thornaby-allocated Class '37' No. 6707 rounds the curve through West Hartlepool station in around 1972 with a Class '9' train of hoppers. It is in corporate blue livery and has lost the 'D' prefix to its number. It was built in 1961 and was to be named *Third East Anglian Regiment* in 1963; nameplates were fitted but never unveiled and they were taken off in September of that year. No. 6707 became No. 37007 in 1974 and then No. 37506 in April 1986 when refurbished and re-geared with CP7 bogies and fitted with a Brush BA1005A main alternator. It was one of twelve of the class refurbished again in 1995 for higher speed operation by fitting former Class '50' bogies for use on the abortive Eurostar 'Nightstar' services over the non-electrified sections of their routes and was renumbered as No. 37604. It was retained by Eurostar for 'Thunderbird' duties until 2007 when it was sold to Direct Rail Services; it is currently (2019) stored out of use at MoD Longtown.

South from West Hartlepool

WD 'Austerity' 2-8-0 No. 90309 with a southbound coal train runs over Bridge Street Level Crossing past Milepost 71¼ on 25th March 1967. In the left distance between the cranes is the Hartlepool Dock Office Clock Tower. No. 90309 was at West Hartlepool from March 1966 until withdrawn in July 1967.

WD 'Austerity' 2-8-0 No. 90116 with a Class '8' coal train alongside the sea wall at West Hartlepool in 1967. It had been transferred there in December 1966 but was withdrawn within six months. In the left background is the former wagon repair works, the trackwork to it having been ripped up.

John Atkinson

English Electric Type '4' No. D385 at Newburn Junction, having departed from West Hartlepool with a southbound express in August 1964. The headcode box appears to be defective, displaying the code '0' for a Light Engine although the rest of the code may be correct with the 'B' signifying a train going to the York District. No. D385 was allocated to York from new in March 1962 until September 1966; it was withdrawn as No. 40185 in August 1982. West Hartlepool shed is on the left, the wagon repair shops are in the centre just to the right of the coaling stage directly below the chimney and the cranes of Hartlepool's docks are visible in the distance. Newburn signal box which was built in 1912 was perched on the sea wall over which an occasional wave would break, soaking whatever was in its path.

CHAPTER 5 - SUNDERLAND TO HARTLEPOOL

WD 'Austerity' 2-8-0 No. 90309 approaching Newburn Bridge on 25th March 1967. It was built by the North British Locomotive Company in February 1944 as WD No. 7445 and received its BR number in November 1951. The tracks in the right foreground lead to West Hartlepool shed.

Peppercorn 'K1' 2-6-0 No. 62004 about to pass under Newburn Bridge towards the engine shed on 17th July 1965. No. 62004 was allocated to West Hartlepool from December 1964 until withdrawn two years later. In the background are the buildings of Newburn Saw Mills and Albion Saw Mills. The wooden sign by the doorway reads 'Ambulance Station 21'.

'Q6' 0-8-0 No. 63421 passes Newburn signal box with another load of pit props conveyed in old NER wooden-bodied wagons in around 1965. It had been at West Hartlepool since L&NER days and lasted until June 1966.

Class '40' No. 259 passes the diesel stabling point on the site of the old West Hartlepool shed in May 1970. Behind it is a Class '37' and an '03' with another '37' in the distance. This is probably a picture of the 'Highwayman', a short-lived bargain fare train from Newcastle to Finsbury Park which was a Class '2' train on a very leisurely schedule via Sunderland and the coastal route. The fare was 35/- single (around £30 in today's prices) and was advertised as 'cheap as a motor coach and over 2 hours faster'.

West Hartlepool shed

There were actually two shed buildings at West Hartlepool, to the south of the site was the roundhouse of traditional NER design and opposite the coaling stage was a three-road running shed. The shed, coded code '51C' from nationalisation, closed to steam on 17th September 1967 and after the buildings were demolished in 1970 the site continued as a diesel stabling point with a couple of shunters and Class '37's parked there at weekends. There were no servicing facilities.

Four residents of the shed at West Hartlepool on 15th June 1952, 'J94' 0-6-0ST No. 68056, 'J73' 0-6-0T, 'J71' 0-6-0T No. 68355 and 'Q6' 0-8-0 No. 63415. At this date the allocation was almost entirely made up of North Eastern Railway classes, including nineteen 'Q6' 0-8-0s, ten 'J26/J27' 0-6-0s, twenty-two 'J71/J72/J73' 0-6-0Ts and for passenger work, two 'D20' 4-4-0s, five 'A8' 4-6-2Ts and six 'G5' 0-4-4Ts. The only modern engines were five 'J94' 0-6-0STs, two 'J39' 0-6-0s and a solitary Ivatt Class '4MT' 2-6-0.

Five 'J94' 0-6-0STs were at West Hartlepool from before nationalisation until 1961 or 1962, and several others arrived in the early 1960s as they were displaced by diesels. No. 68051, standing in front of the coaling stage on 25th August 1962, had been transferred from York in October 1955 along with No. 68021 from Heaton; it stayed on until April 1964.

An LM&SR design amongst the Eastern engines, Ivatt Class '4MT' 2-6-0 No. 43123 on 25th August 1962. A wonderful display of pipework and rodding including AWS fittings. It must have been cold and wet that August in the north east to need a cover between engine and tender! No. 43123 was built at Horwich and entered service in August 1951 at Selby where it stayed until September 1959 moving to Hull Dairycoates for two years before arriving at West Hartlepool in June 1961; it stayed until April 1966 moving to York.

'B1' 4-6-0 No. 61061, also on 25th August 1962, was at West Hartlepool from October 1958 until November 1962 and increased the shed's allocation of the class to three, which remained the case until late 1962.

'Q6' 0-8-0 No. 63440 at West Hartlepool on 25th August 1962 was built by Armstrong, Whitworth in 1920 as NER No. 2283. It had been transferred to West Hartlepool in October 1958 from Stockton and ended its days there in December 1966.

A contrast in tank engines in the roundhouse at West Hartlepool on 25th August 1962. It is difficult to believe that the 'J72' on the left is the newer of the two engines, entering service in April 1951, compared to 'J94' 0-6-0ST No. 68056 which had been built by Bagnalls for the War Department in late 1945 and was acquired by the L&NER in October 1946. No. 68056 was at West Hartlepool until its withdrawal in October 1962, but No. 69021 only arrived in August 1961 after ten years at Darlington; it lasted almost a year longer and was not taken out of service until September 1963.

After the design was selected, essentially by default because it was the only contender, as the L&NER standard light shunting engine after the Second World War, twenty-eight of what was basically Worsdell's 1898 North Eastern Railway 0-6-0T were built by British Railways between 1949 and 1951. One of these was No. 69003 which came to West Hartlepool from York in November 1961 and was withdrawn from there in December 1963 along with classmates Nos. 69011 and 69019.

Thompson 'B1' 4-6-0 No. 61220 at rest in 1965 with the tender of an Ivatt '4MT' 2-6-0 peeking out of the shed. It was built by NBL for the L&NER and entered service in August 1947 at Stockton. It only had two more sheds, Thornaby from June 1959 to March 1963, and finally West Hartlepool until withdrawn in October 1965.

CHAPTER 5 - SUNDERLAND TO HARTLEPOOL

Dereliction has set in at West Hartlepool in Summer 1967, with what appear to be three withdrawn engines, two 'Austerities' and 'Q6' No. 63407 which was taken out of service at the end of June. During the last few days of steam working in September, the main duties were coal trains up to the pits on the coast and on the Wellfield line worked by 'Q6' 0-8-0s and 'Austerities', together with local trip workings.

Three railwaymen have a chat in the sunshine in front of a line of withdrawn Hunslet 0-6-0 204bhp diesel shunters in August 1967. No. D2591 on the right and the other three Hunslets on the shed's books had been taken out of service in March. WD 2-8-0 No. 90677 had just been transferred from Hull Dairycoates together with three classmates, replacing other members of the class that had been withdrawn the previous month. *John Atkinson*

6 – Teesside

The area around the estuary of the River Tees became heavily industrialised from the 1850s onwards after ironstone was discovered in the Cleveland Hills, and the railways grew to match. They brought in raw materials such as coal and ore and transported iron and steel products out from the many works and factories. There were extensive sidings on the south of the River to handle this traffic and several major steam sheds were built to handle the large number of freight engines which worked there.

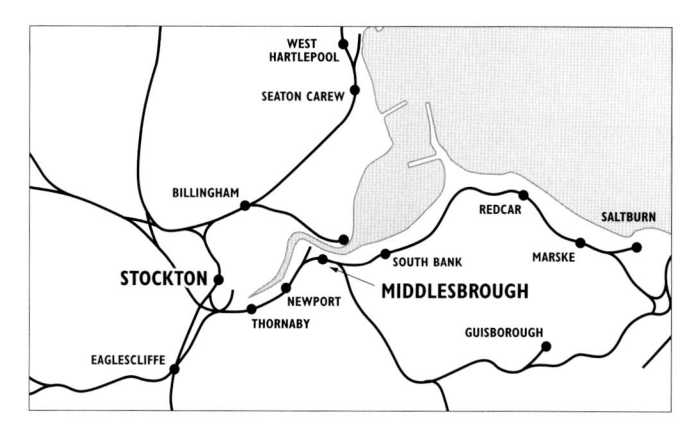

Seaton Carew

Peppercorn 'K1' 2-6-0 No. 62023 with empty hoppers at Seaton Carew in the pouring rain in 1966. The station is still open today with an hourly service in both directions. This picture was probably taken while No. 62023 was allocated to Sunderland, between June and October 1966.

Billingham

BR Sulzer Type '2 No. D5112 leaving the I.C.I. works at Billingham on 19th March 1963 with a train load of 350 tons of iso-octanol, a plasticiser alcohol, for shipment to Australia. The liquid will be pumped from the 27½-ton tank wagons, which had been specially designed for this traffic, directly into tanks on board the ship. No. D5112 was built at Darlington in December 1960 and was in its second spell at Gateshead, between the end of 1961 and June 1964. It was transferred to Scotland in late 1971, renumbered to No. 24112 in 1974 and withdrawn at the end of 1976.

Billingham station looking towards Stockton on 12th May 1965. An English Electric Type '3' and brake tender is running through the Up platform and will pass under the A19 Billingham Station By-Pass. The station was closed in November 1966.
Ben Brooksbank

A lady waits with her baby in a pushchair at the level crossing as English Electric Type '3' No. D6776 brings a long train of small coal westwards through Billingham on 13th September 1967. It will probably have come down from the West Hartlepool line which met the line from Middlesbrough at Billingham Junction which is just out of sight at the rear of the train. No. D6776 was built at the Robert Stephenson & Hawthorns Works in October 1962 and was allocated to Thornaby until late 1972. It became No. 37086 in 1974 and then No. 37518 in June 1987 after it was refurbished and re-geared with CP7 bogies and fitted with a Brush BA1005A main alternator. It was purchased by West Coast Railways, the spot hire company and charter train operator, in 2011 and is still operational.

Middlesbrough

A view from the shed on 9th June 1953 as 'J26' 0-6-0 No. 65754 shunts Iron Ore wagons and a 'Q6' passes under the signal gantry on the right. No. 65754 was built in 1905 and was at Newport shed until closure but it did not survive the subsequent transfer to Thornaby and was withdrawn immediately. It was passing in front of the cargo ship *Clan Allan* which had been built for the Ministry of War Transport in 1942 by J.Readhead & Sons Ltd at South Shields and served during the war as *Empire Forest*. It was bought as a temporary stop-gap by Clan Line Steamers Ltd in 1946 whilst replacements were built to replace the company's wartime losses and was renamed *Clan Allan*, working for the company until 1958.

Fairburn '4MT' 2-6-4T No. 42085 working a Darlington to Saltburn train at Guisborough Junction, just east of Middlesbrough station on 13th June 1954. No. 42085 was built at Brighton in 1951 and was one of three of the LM&SR designed 2-6-4Ts transferred from the Southern Region in early 1952. Initially, it went to Heaton but soon moved to Darlington, in July, and stayed there until September 1955 when it left for Scarborough. No. 42085 is now preserved at the Lakeside & Haverthwaite Railway.

BR built 'J72' 0-6-0T No. 69006 passes Dock Hill signal box as it approaches the station with a train of BR-built 'Boplate' bogie plate wagons, which were used to carry sheet steel, in August 1956. It was allocated to Middlesbrough shed from new in November 1949 until the shed closed in June 1958 and it went to Thornaby.

'Q6' 0-8-0 No. 63389 trundles past the station towards Newport with a very mixed selection of wagons in tow, ranging from new 16T steel mineral wagons to former NER wooden opens, in June 1956. The 1917-built 0-8-0 was at Newport from April 1947 until the shed closed in 1958 and after 3½ years at Thornaby ended its days at Tyne Dock.

'A8' 4-6-2T No. 69860 acting as Middlesbrough station pilot is shunting a single Gresley-designed L&NER full brake. The picture was taken while it was allocated to Middlesbrough, between June 1957 and June 1958. No. 69860 was built in 1913 as a NER 'H1' 4-4-4T and was rebuilt into a 4-6-2T in 1934.

Saltburn 'A8' 4-6-2T No. 69869 after arrival with a local at Middlesbrough on 24th July 1956. DMUs took over the Middlesbrough-Saltburn-Whitby-Scarborough services in May 1958, the six 'A8's at Saltburn having been transferred to Middlesbrough in February 1958. No. 69869 has a caged-pattern bunker and a later boiler with cladding of a smaller diameter than the smokebox.

CHAPTER 6 - TEESSIDE

'J26' 0-6-0 No. 65745 with yet another load of steel girders passes Middlesbrough East signal box on 31st March 1959 as the lone spotter checks his ABC. A tank engine of either class 'J71' or 'J72' shunts the sidings to the left and a DMU is held in the sidings on the right. As with Sunderland, there were no totem signs and the station name was printed on the light diffusers. No. 65745 was allocated to Newport until it closed in June 1958 and was then transferred to Thornaby where it worked until withdrawn in December 1961.

Thornaby

At the eastern end of Thornaby station in a picture taken from beside the signal box, 'J26' 0-6-0 No. 65770 takes a freight towards Middlesbrough on 11th August 1956. The 1905 Gateshead-built engine was at Newport shed from nationalisation until closure in June 1958.

A more modern L&NER-built 0-6-0, 'J39' No. 64942 from Sunderland shed runs through on the freight line in a picture taken in the same direction, but from the platform, on 24th August 1960. Note the prominent sign for 'M. Henderson Clark', scrap metal merchants at their premises behind the goods yard.

Thornaby Depot

On 5 June 1958 the new Motive Power Depot at Thornaby was formally opened. Costing £1,250,000, it was built on a 70-acre site to the east of Thornaby station at the west end of the Newport yards. The depot replaced two old sheds at Middlesbrough and Newport and of the initial allocation of 148 steam locomotives, sixty-two engines came from Middlesbrough and eighty-six from Newport.

The depot was built to handle steam locomotives initially but was designed so that it could easily be converted to house diesel locomotives. The two main buildings consisted of a straight shed and repair shop, and a round-house. The straight shed was double-ended with six roads, 265ft long; under the same roof, although separated from the straight shed by a wall, was the five-road repair shop. The round-house, the last such built for British Railways, was an octagonal structure built round a 70ft electric turntable with twenty-two stalls plus two inlet/outlet roads. On the north side of the depot there were five covered preparation pits and four covered inspection pits, with wet ash-pit accommodation for sixteen locomotives at the west end of the inspection pits. There was a 350-ton mechanical coaling plant, capable of coaling four locomotives simultaneously and the whole of the east end of the depot was spanned by a gantry carrying water and sand mains to deliver directly to a locomotive beneath. The layout was carefully planned around the sequence of operations between a locomotive's entrance and its departure from the depot and allowed for a locomotive to bypass any or all of the disposal operations not required and return to traffic in the shortest possible time. Thornaby was closed to steam in December 1964 and completely in 2009; the buildings were demolished in 2011.

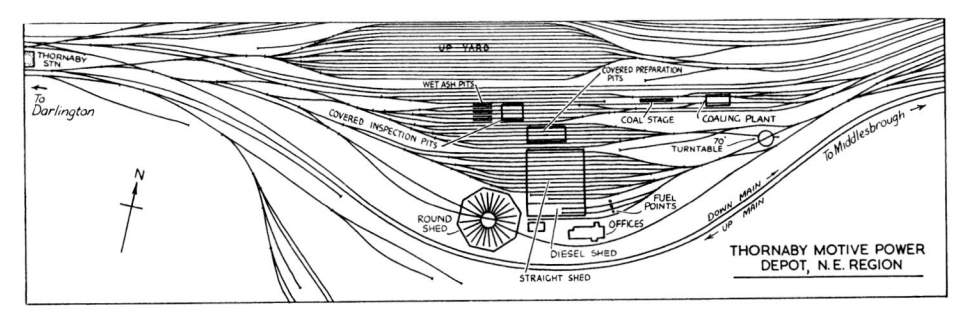

The round-house was an octagonal structure about 100 yards in diameter, built around a 70ft electric turntable. It had twenty-two stalls plus two inlet/outlet roads.

At the west end of the yard was a 350-ton mechanical coaling plant, capable of coaling four locomotives simultaneously. It had three hoppers which were filled by raising wagons bodily in a cradle to the top of the structure. Both wagon and cradle were then lifted out of the guides and traversed to whichever of the hoppers was to be replenished, and the wagon tipped to discharge its contents. Engine crews controlled the four feeders from the hoppers by push buttons. In an attempt to reduce breakage of the soft South Durham coal, the open-topped hoppers sloped gently down towards the chutes. The operator in the lifting cabin could move a wagon horizontally across the top of the hopper before tilting and emptying it.

'L1' 2-6-4T No. 67754, 'J71' 0-6-0T No. 68272 and another 'J71' in front of the coaling plant on 25th September 1960. The water tower on the left held 200,000 gallons and had fifteen distribution points. The yard was lit by three-lamp clusters mounted on 50ft high steel towers. The depot was built alongside the modernised Tees Marshalling Yard which is visible in the background.

A number of 350bhp diesel-electric shunters were transferred from Darlington to the new depot. Two of them were in the small diesel maintenance shop in the south-east corner of the straight shed. No. 13139 had arrived at Thornaby from Darlington in July 1958 and was withdrawn from there in June 1968, having been renumbered to D3139 in September 1958. It was built in March 1955 and was one of 161 British Railways 350bhp 0-6-0 diesel shunters built with a Lister-Blackstone ER6T engine and GEC traction motors instead of the more common English Electric 6KT engine and transmission. Although classed as '10' under TOPS they were all withdrawn under the National Traction Plan as non-standard, without renumbering.

CHAPTER 6 - TEESSIDE 155

Two 'J50' 0-6-0Ts, Nos. 68942 and 68948, at the head of a line of nine 0-6-0Ts of all four types, classes 'J71/J72/J50/J94', which moved to the new depot in 1958. No. 69842 was withdrawn in September 1958 and No. 68948 left in December, and all the others had gone by the end of 1963. Above them is the roof of the covered inspection pits and to the right of these are the covered preparation pits.

The new depot was designed to handle up to 220 locomotives and the 148 transferred at the opening date were added to when Stockton and Haverton Hill (near Billingham) sheds were closed in June 1959. Two thirds of the initial allocation was made up of freight engines, thirty-four 'Q6' 0-8-0s, thirty 'WD' 2-8-0s and forty-four 0-6-0s of 'J25', 'J26' and 'J27'; there were four Ivatt Class '4' 2-6-0s. From left to right are 'Austerity' No. 90479 which had been transferred from Haverton Hill, Ivatt No. 43057 which was in its second spell at the shed arriving from York in February 1961 and 'Q6' No. 63428 which came from Newport in June 1958.

Named 'B1' 4-6-0 No. 61241 *Viscount Ridley* inside the octagonal shed on the 70ft electrically-operated turntable. Thornaby acquired eleven of the class from Stockton and Haverton Hill in June 1959 but No. 61241 was not among these and was from Blaydon.

'Austerity' 2-8-0 No. 90048 on the turntable in the round-house on 25th September 1960. It had been transferred to Thornaby in August 1959 from West Hartlepool and was there until withdrawn in May 1963. It had been built by the North British Locomotive Company in 1944 and was taken into L&NER stock in February 1947 as No. 3048, becoming No. 63048 in May 1948 and finally No. 90048 in October 1950.

English Electric Type '3' No. D6769 at the depot on 6th October 1962 was allocated to Thornaby for thirty years, from new in July 1962 until May 1992. It became No. 37069 under TOPS and was given the name *Thornaby TMD* on 1986. It went to France in July 1999 and returned in October 2000; it was withdrawn in May 2001.

The penultimate English Electric Type '4' No. D398, which entered service in August 1962, in front of the six road straight shed. This picture was taken during the first of two spells when it was allocated to Thornaby, from September 1962 to June 1963. The pristine brake tender, No. B964077E, was built at York in 1963 to Diagram 1/555 and weighed 35 tons, most of which was scrap or concrete ballast. Most of the tenders of this type were fitted with Gresley 8ft 6in double bolster bogies as illustrated here.

The Clayton Type '1' Bo-Bo was one of British Railways' most unsuccessful diesel classes and although intended as the new standard Type '1' when introduced in 1962, they were all withdrawn by the end of 1971. Thornaby was the first depot on the NER to receive an allocation when Nos. D8588-D8591 arrived from Beyer, Peacock in 1964 and one of these is pictured there during that year; all four were transferred to Gateshead in 1966. However, Gateshead offloaded five of them onto Thornaby in February 1969, but they returned to Tyneside in 1969/70.

The east end of the depot was spanned by a gantry carrying water and sand mains. Water supply pipes were suspended from the gantry and the supply could be controlled by a fireman from the tender top of his engine. The sand supply was blown automatically from hoppers in the sand house to flexible pipes suspended from the gantry; all that the fireman had to do was to take a cap off the pipe, hold the nozzle over the sandbox on the locomotive and turn a small lever, whereupon a supply of fine dry sand was delivered.

Newport

One of the massive 'T1' 4-8-0Ts designed for hump shunting, No. 69922 in the yard at Newport on 27th April 1954. Ten were built by the NER in 1909/10 and a further five by the L&NER in 1925, including No. 69922 which was allocated to Newport until September 1955 when it was transferred to Stockton. In the background is the famous transporter bridge linking Middlesbrough with Port Clarence on the north bank of the Tees. It was built in 1911, has a span of 590ft, is the oldest remaining transporter bridge in the world and was granted Grade II listed status in 1985. *H.C. Casserley*

Inside one of the three roundhouses at Newport shed on 15th August 1954 with four 'Q6' 0-8-0s visible, including Nos. 63347, 63345 and 63430 which were all allocated there. On the right there is an unidentified 'J94' 0-6-0ST and 'T1' 4-8-0T No. 69922. The shed which was opened by the NER in 1875 was closed in June 1958 when the new Thornaby Depot opened and its eighty-six locomotives transferred there. *Walter Dendy - BW Brooksbank collection*

South Bank

South Bank was two miles east of Middlesbrough on the line to Redcar and Saltburn. The NER McKenzie & Holland gantry indicates the complex trackwork on the heavily used freight lines in the area. One of Newport shed's extensive fleet of almost forty 'J26' 0-6-0s, No. 65774, backs through on 9th June 1953. All except a couple of them survived long enough to be transferred to Thornaby when the shed closed in 1958. In the background it is just possible to discern part of the Cargo Fleet steelworks.

Stockton

'A3' 4-6-2 No. 60072 *Sunstar* arriving at Stockton with a southbound express in the mid-1950s. Unlike Gateshead, Heaton shed kept its Pacifics clean and No. 60072 proves that its engines did not always work north from Newcastle. The train could well be the 7.43am from Sunderland to King's Cross which was a regular Heaton working as far as Peterborough up until the early 1960s. Most of its Pacific stud were 'A3's which usually worked this train between 1955 and 1960, although occasionally one of the shed's 'V2's was used. *Sunstar* was at Heaton until October 1958, when it moved to Tweedmouth, but returned in July 1961 and was there until withdrawal in October 1962.

Stockton shed on 13th June 1954, a quiet Sunday afternoon. The signal box in the left background is North Shore on the main line to West Hartlepool. The shed provided motive power mainly for the intensive freight traffic in the Teesside area and in 1954 had an allocation of fifty-three:- eleven 4-6-0s, fifteen 2-8-0s (all ex-WD), three 2-6-0s, five 0-8-0s, five 0-6-0s, one 4-8-0T, two 4-6-2Ts, four 0-6-0Ts, six 0-4-4Ts and one 0-4-0T. Five of the 4-6-0s were named 'B1's which were used on fitted freight work to York and March. The shed was closed in June 1959, a year later than planned, and its allocation transferred to the new Thornaby Depot which had opened the previous year. *Ben Brooksbank*

One of the three 4-8-0Ts employed at Stockton for hump-shunting in the marshalling yard resting on a Sunday in the shed yard on 13th June 1954. These NER class 'X' (L&NER 'T1') 4-8-0Ts were introduced by Wilson Worsdell in 1909 and more were built after Grouping; No. 69919 was built in November 1925 as No. 657, became L&NER No. 9919 in 1946 and survived until February 1955. *Ben Brooksbank*

Thompson 'L1' 2-6-2T No. 67763 runs light through Stockton in the late 1950s. It was built by the North British Locomotive Company in January 1949 and spent its early years mostly at Hull Dairycoates before moving north to Middlesbrough and Whitby and then on to Darlington from September 1957 until November 1961.

An Immingham Brush Type '4' with what was recorded as a southbound fish train, No. D1870 passes through Stockton on 20th May 1969. It spent two years at Tinsley before transferring to Immingham in September 1967 and stayed there until 1982 when it moved to Thornaby. No. D1870 had been built at the Brush Falcon Works in Loughborough in March 1964 and was withdrawn in 1994 as No. 47220.

Eaglescliffe

The Stephenson Locomotive Society and Manchester Locomotive Society organised the 'Northern Dales Rail Tour' from Manchester Victoria on 4th September 1955. 'A8' 4-6-2T No. 69855 took the tour from Darlington North Road to Northallerton via Eaglescliffe, where it was photographed, and back to Northallerton.

In the mid-1950s there were over thirty trains daily each way between Darlington and Saltburn/Middlesbrough. 'A8' 4-6-2T No. 69870 is leaving Eaglescliffe with a Darlington-Saltburn working, probably soon after completing a General repair at Darlington Works in September 1953. It was allocated to West Auckland from 1940 until June 1958, moving to Sunderland for its last two years in service. No. 69870 has the original pattern of bunker with conventional coal rails rather than the 'cage' type fitted in later years to many of the class.

Sedgefield

Thornaby 'Q6' 0-8-0 No. 63428 on a southbound train of empty 16T steel mineral wagons near Sedgefield on 28th September 1960. It was one of the class built by Armstrong, Whitworth for the North Eastern Railway, entering service in 1920 as No. 2271.

English Electric Type '3' No. D6772 at Mordon just to the west of Sedgefield on the line from Ferryhill to Stockton with a southbound coal train on 6th May 1964. It had been built at Robert Stephenson & Hawthorn in September 1962 and was at Thornaby until early 1970. No. D6772 was renumbered as No. 37072 under TOPS in 1974 and was withdrawn in January 1999.

7 – Malton to Pickering and the North Yorkshire Moors

The line from York to Scarborough via Malton and Seamer was built by George Hudson's York & North Midland Railway and opened in 1845. A branch to Pickering which left the Scarborough line at Rillington was opened at the same time. The York & North Midland Railway completed its route to Whitby by taking over the Whitby & Pickering Railway, which is still in existence today as the North Yorkshire Moors Railway between Pickering and Grosmont with running powers into Whitby over the Network Rail line. Passenger services were withdrawn in September 1930 from all intermediate stations between York and Scarborough except Malton and Seamer in order to speed up traffic between York and Scarborough.

Malton

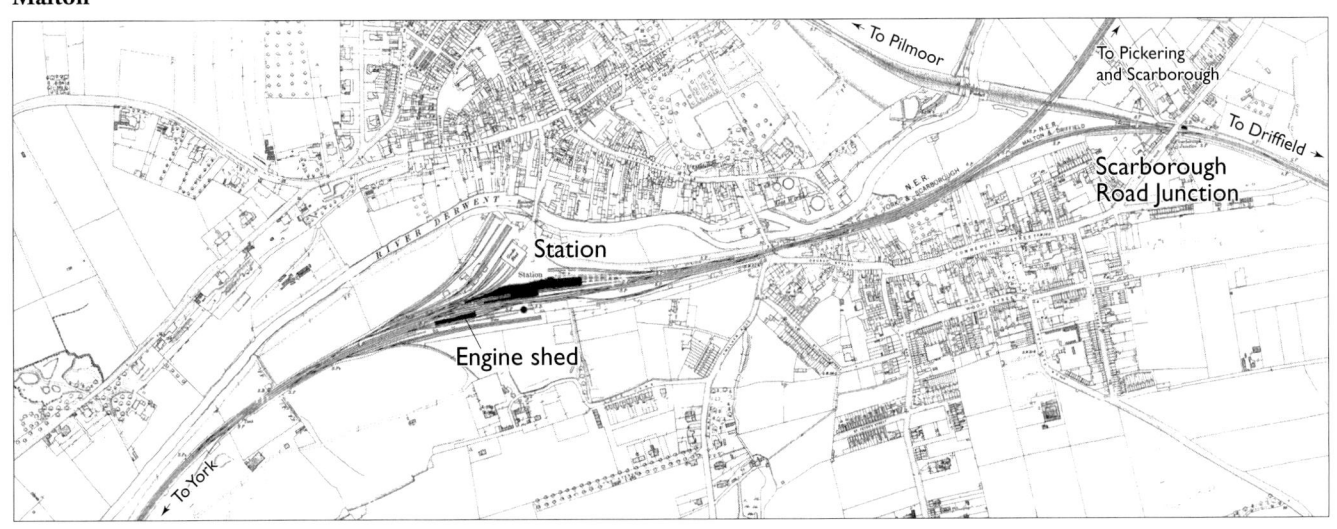

In May 1853 Malton became a junction when the Malton & Driffield Railway and the Thirsk & Malton Railway opened, the latter leaving the East Coast main line at Pilmoor and meeting with the Malton & Driffield at Scarborough Road Junction east of Malton station. The only access to the station was via an east to south curve which meant that trains between Malton to Pilmoor had to run past the junction and then reverse. The Driffield line was closed to passenger traffic in June 1950 and completely in October 1958 but the Pilmoor line lasted until 1963.

'B16/1' 4-6-0 No. 61423 passes the shed as it arrives at Malton with a train for Scarborough in the early 1950s. Two of the shed's 'G5' 0-4-4Ts are in the background; the one nearest the camera is No. 67308 which was allocated there but sub-shedded at Pickering from February 1953 until withdrawn in November 1955. No. 61423 was allocated to York from before nationalisation until withdrawal in September 1961.
Kenneth Field/Rail Archive Stephenson

The first engine shed at Malton was built in 1853 and extended in 1867; it had a sub-shed at Pickering. At its peak in the 1930s it had eighteen engines on its books but the number by this date was around a dozen. It had code 50F under British Railways and closed in April 1963. This 1958 picture has examples of three of the four classes allocated there at that time. In the shed is a 'J39' 0-6-0 and outside on the left 'A8' 4-6-2T No. 69861 which was allocated there from June 1956 until withdrawn four years later; on the right is 'G5' 0-4-4T No. 67342 which had arrived from Sunderland in March 1958 but was withdrawn at the end of the year.

Watched by a typical 1950s trainspotter complete with cycle clips on his trousers, 'B1' 4-6-0 No. 61013 *Topi* runs through with an excursion from Leeds to the coast in 1959. It was built in December 1946 at Darlington and spent its first decade at Gateshead before moving to Ardsley in October 1956, staying there until November 1965. The first forty-one 'B1's were all named after antelopes and Topi, also called Tsessebe or Sassaby, were one of Africa's most common antelopes.

Another Ardsley 'B1' on an eastbound excursion, No. 61110, rushes through the deserted platforms of Malton station. It was built at the same time as No. 61013, but by the North British Locomotive Company. After spending its early years mostly at former Great Central sheds, it moved to the ex-Great Northern shed at Leeds in January 1952 and stayed until withdrawn in October 1965. The station had a solid overall roof and an unusual layout with two platform faces on a single running line. This dated from 1862 when the station was expanded and the Up island platform was built outside the wall which supported the overall roof. Instead of a footbridge or subway to provide access from the station building on the right to the new platform, a novel and much cheaper solution was employed. A removable section of platform, in the form of a wheeled trolley running on rails set at right-angles to the running line, was used. When a train had to use the platform, the trolley was wheeled back under the Up platform. The trolley was interlocked with the signals controlling access to the platform.

CHAPTER 7 - MALTON TO PICKERING AND THE NORTH YORKSHIRE MOORS

Gresley 'K3' 2-6-0 No. 61839 leans into the curve as yet another coast bound excursion roars through Malton in 1959. No.61839 was allocated to Mexborough from February to July 1959 which narrows down the date of this picture. There was an extensive goods yard at Malton and some of the buildings and the water tank are visible on the right. The station is still in use today, albeit with only the single platform on the right of the train and was given Grade II listed status in 1986.

An enthusiasts' party stops to record the engines on shed on Saturday 13th April 1957. At this date the shed's allocation comprised two 'A8' 4-6-2Ts, four 'G5' 0-4-4Ts, four 'J27' 0-6-0s and four 'J39' 0-6-0s. 'J39' No. 64938 had been there since April 1954 and 'G5' No. 67315, peeping out of the shed, since April 1956.

An illustration of an unusual manoeuvre caused by the track layout to the east of Malton station. Ivatt 2-6-2T No. 41265 is crossing Bridge 15 on the Malton to Scarborough line, looking north towards Scarborough. The train which it is coupled up to had come from Scarborough, and had previously passed under this bridge and stopped in Malton station. The station pilot, No. 41265, was then attached at the rear and hauled the complete train backwards up the connecting spur from the station to Scarborough Road Junction on the Driffield to Pilmoor line. After No. 41265 had been uncoupled, the train could proceed to Pilmoor where it would gain access to the northbound East Coast main line. This was a regular movement for holiday trains from Scarborough to the North East and Scotland, avoiding reversal at the busy York station. No. 41265 was one of three of the LM&SR-designed tanks transferred to Malton to replace the shed's 'G5' 0-4-4Ts in January 1959; it stayed until withdrawal in December 1962.

CHAPTER 7 - MALTON TO PICKERING AND THE NORTH YORKSHIRE MOORS

Pickering

NER 'G5' 0-4-4T No. 67273 stands at Pickering with the 8.35am push and pull train from Seamer after taking water on 5th June and No. 67273 worked the last train, the 6.40pm from Scarborough to Pickering on 3rd June. It was built at Darlington in 1896 as NER No. 1737, renumbered to L&NER No. 7273 in April 1946 and No. 67273 in July 1948, and was allocated to Malton until October 1950 when it was transferred to Darlington. Pickering is now the southern terminus of the line which formerly connected at Rillington with the Malton to Scarborough line, and is of course now the administrative headquarters of the North Yorkshire Moors Railway.
A.W. Croughton/Rail Archive Stephenson

BR Standard Class '4' 2-6-4T No. 80117 on a northbound train at Pickering while allocated to Whitby; it was there from new in June 1955 until June 1958 when it moved to Leeds Neville Hill. Whitby had five of the class in the mid-1950s and they were used on services to Malton, York, Scarborough, Stockton and Middlesbrough. The overall roof designed by G. T. Andrews, which was similar to the one at Malton, had been removed in 1953 but the North Yorkshire Moors Railway reinstated it in 2011.

Three enthusiasts walk back to the station after viewing the 'G5' 0-4-4T tucked away in Pickering shed on 13th April 1957. The single track shed built in 1846 was extended from 43ft to 112ft in the 1870s. It was a sub-shed of Malton and was closed in April 1959.

A BR-built 204bhp 0-6-0 diesel shunter, later Class '03', runs through Pickering station. It was continuing the L&NER tradition of using small shunting locomotives to work up a line, shunting each yard, in order to minimise the work for the pick-up goods.

The North Yorkshire Moors line

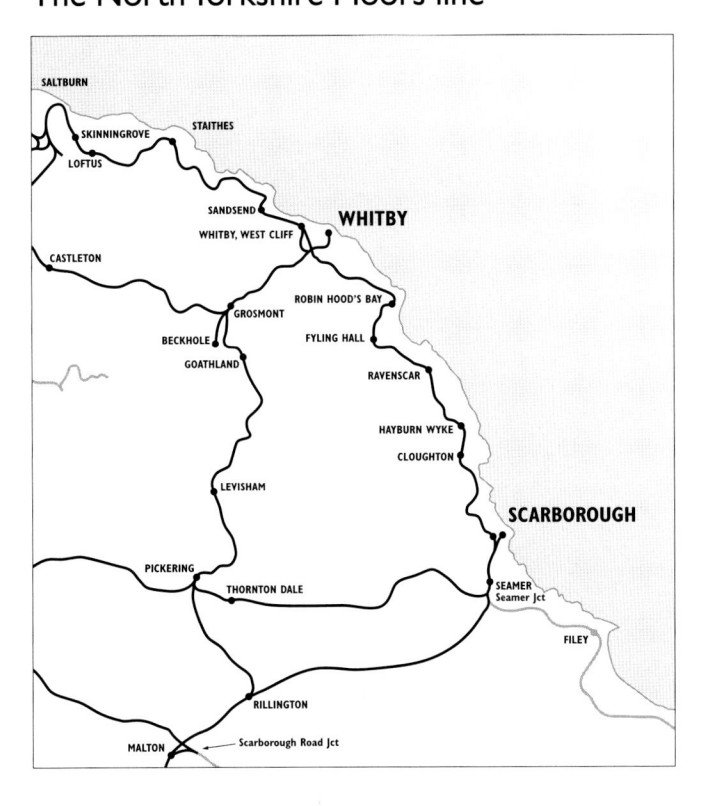

The railway between Pickering and Whitby opened in 1836 with horses providing the motive power, helped by a section of rope haulage over the 1 in 10 gradient between Beck Hole and Goathland. The Whitby & Pickering Railway was taken over by George Hudson's York & North Midland Railway, the embryonic North Eastern Railway, in 1844 and the line was upgraded to allow steam power to take over from the horses by 1847. The rope operation ended in 1865 when a 4½ mile long deviation line was opened, albeit still with a 1 in 49 gradient. The line runs through the magnificent scenery of the North York Moors National Park.

The Malton-Whitby passenger service was withdrawn on 6th March 1965 and the line between Pickering and Grosmont was closed. In June 1967 when it appeared that track lifting was about to begin, a meeting was held to discuss the possible re-opening of the line and in November the North Yorkshire Moors Railway Preservation Society held its inaugural meeting. By 1969 the Society was able to pay a deposit to British Rail to secure the future of the line and in 1971 a Draft Light Railway Order was transferred over to the Preservation Society. Public services commenced between Grosmont and Pickering and two years later were extended into Pickering station. After three decades of steady progress, the NYMR gained a train operator's Passenger Licence and an access contract with Network Rail was signed to allow it to operate trains through from Grosmont to Whitby on Network Rail metals, and today there is a daily service between Pickering and Whitby.

Levisham

'A8' 4-6-2T No. 69877 leaving Levisham with a train to Whitby. It was allocated to Malton from June 1953 until October 1956 and for six months in 1957. No. 69877 was rebuilt from a NER 'H1' 4-4-4T in 1934; it was withdrawn from Scarborough at the end of 1959.

Fairburn 2-6-4T No. 42083 starting up Newtondale bank having just left Levisham on a train to Whitby. It was built at Brighton in February 1951 for the Southern Region but was transferred to the North Eastern Region in early 1952. The NER was waiting for delivery of three new BR Standard 2-6-4Ts and to fill the gap, three Fairburn 2-6-4Ts, Nos. 42083-42085, were transferred in their place. No. 42083 moved to Whitby in September 1955 and was followed by No. 42084 and 42085 in February 1956; all three left in April 1959 after DMUs had taken over the Malton to Whitby trains. The composition of the train is interesting with two 'blood and custard' liveried coaches at the front, a L&NER Thompson brake third followed by a BR Mark 1, and then five ex-NER coaches and a fish van at the tail end! The first vehicle which has destination boards is probably the single coach Whitby portion of the 'Scarborough Flyer'.

Beckhole – climbing to Grosmont

Ivatt Class '2' 2-6-2T No. 41251 and 'B1' 4-6-0 No. 61112 climb from Grosmont near Beckhole with an Up train in c1960. No. 41251 had been transferred to Malton in January 1959 along with classmates Nos. 41252 and 41265 to replace three withdrawn 'G5' 0-4-4Ts. The 'B1' was from Sheffield Darnall where it was shedded between May 1959 and December 1962. The Malton 2-6-2Ts were regularly used as pilots on the summer excursions to Scarborough and Whitby.
Cecil Ord/Rail Archive Stephenson

Grosmont

On the final day of the mammoth SLS/RCTS 'North Eastern Tour' on 1st October 1963, two named 'B1' 4-6-0s were used. The day's activities started at Whitby and ended at York. No. 61021 *Reitbok* which had brought the party from Malton has drawn the train forwards out of Grosmont station and No. 61031 *Reedbuck* is about couple on to the rear of the train for the journey tender-first to Battersby.

A Metropolitan-Cammell DMU on a Malton to Whitby service at Grosmont in around 1964; the service ended on 6th March 1965. Grosmont, which is 18 miles from Pickering, is where today's heritage railway meets the main line rail network. It is a junction with the Esk Valley Line to Battersby which is just visible on the left between the signal box and the DMU.

8 – To the seaside – Whitby and Scarborough

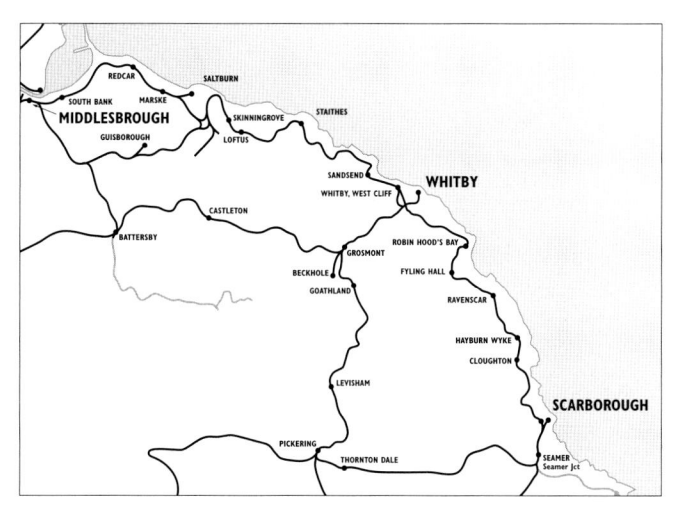

The railway between Middlesbrough and Whitby and down the coast to Scarborough developed in a piecemeal fashion. There were two routes between Middlesbrough and Loftus, one inland via Guisborough and one along the coast built by the Stockton & Darlington Railway through Redcar and Marske, that originally terminated at Saltburn, but reached Loftus via a new connection to Brotton where it met the line from Guisborough. The line south from Loftus down the coast to Whitby had a chequered history. It was started by the Whitby, Redcar & Middlesbrough Union Railway in 1871 but was only completed in 1883 after the North Eastern Railway took over, with much of the line having to be reconstructed because of the poor standard of work by the original contractor who went into liquidation in 1874. When the Loftus to Whitby line closed in May 1958, trains from Middlesbrough to Whitby and Scarborough had to use the inland Esk Valley line via Battersby and Grosmont.

Middlesbrough to Whitby along the coast

Marske

Ivatt '4MT' No. 43054 seems to be doing most of the work as it banks Newport shed's 'Q6' 0-8-0 No. 63370 on a Class '8' freight at Marske on 1st July 1954. The LM&SR designed 2-6-0 was allocated to Middlesbrough but would move to Saltburn later in the month; No. 63370 was at Newport until the shed's allocation was transferred wholesale to the new Thornaby Depot in June 1958.

The last of the L&NER batch of 'A5/2' 4-6-2Ts, No. 69842, which was built by Hawthorn, Leslie and entered service in March 1926. It was working a Saltburn to Darlington train at Marske on 1st July 1954 and had been shedded at Darlington since July 1951.

A LM&SR-designed engine built at Brighton in 1951 for the Southern Region working a Saltburn to Darlington train on the North Eastern Region at Marske on 16th July 1954. Fairburn 2-6-4T No. 42084 had been transferred to the NER in March 1952 but retains evidence of its Southern days in the form of the additional lamp irons half-way down the smokebox rim, which were fitted to carry that Region's headcode discs. It had been allocated to Darlington since April 1952 and spent the second half of the 1950s at either Whitby or Scarborough, up until it went to Low Moor in April 1959.

Saltburn

The station was opened by the Stockton and Darlington Railway as the terminus of their line from Redcar in 1861. Eleven years later, the North Eastern Railway opened a line towards Brotton from the town, but this diverged from the original route some 440 yards west of the station. This meant the passenger trains from the town to Loftus and Whitby had to reverse into and out of the terminus before regaining the correct direction at Saltburn West Junction. This line is still in operation today to serve the Skinningrove steelworks and the Boulby potash mine, although passenger trains ceased in 1951.

'A8' 4-6-2T No. 69884 at Saltburn on the 11.55am to Darlington in the mid-1950s. It was rebuilt from a 4-4-4T in June 1933 and was allocated to Saltburn from 1939 until November 1957 and has the later style of modified bunker with 'cage'-type coal rails. It is difficult to believe that in the mid-1950s there were over thirty trains daily each way between Saltburn and Darlington. Saltburn had developed rapidly as a seaside resort in the mid-19th Century partly as a result of the line built by the Stockton & Darlington Railway to the town which was completed in 1861.

CHAPTER 8 - TO THE SEASIDE - WHITBY AND SCARBOROUGH

A Hughes-Fowler 'Crab' 2-6-0 from Sheffield Grimesthorpe is re-coaled at Saltburn shed, probably after working in with an excursion or a Redcar Races special, on 17th September 1955. No. 42794 spent over twenty years at the Sheffield shed, in three spells, finally leaving for the former Lancashire & Yorkshire Railway shed at Wigan in July 1961. The original 1864 shed behind the tender of No. 42794 could accommodate only two engines and an extension, off to the right of this picture, was built in 1877 to accommodate four more engines; the shed closed in 1958.

Skinningrove

English Electric Type '3' No. D6778 waits in front of the Skinningrove Iron Company works as the guard rounds up the stragglers who are hurrying back to the RCTS 'North Eastern No. 3 Railtour' on 6th May 1967. The tour started at Bradford Exchange and the train was worked from there to Middlesbrough by 'Jubilee' No. 45562 *Alberta* which handed over to No. D6778 there. It took the party to Redcar before returning to Middlesbrough via Saltburn. No. D6778 was allocated to Thornaby from new in October 1962 until October 1971 when it moved to March. It was renumbered as No. 37078 under TOPS and was named *Teesside Steelmaster* in 1984.

Loftus

In typical North Yorkshire weather, BR Standard 2-6-4T No. 80117 at Loftus with a train to Whitby, probably in 1957. It was allocated to Whitby from new in May 1955 until ousted by DMUs in June 1958 when it moved to Neville Hill replacing that shed's 'D49' 4-4-0s and 'B1' 4-6-0s on local services from Leeds along with the other four of the class from Whitby, Nos. 80116, 80118-80120.

Staithes

No. 80117 at Staithes with a train to Whitby in April 1957, possibly on the same day as the above picture. On the extreme left is a camping coach, several of which could be found between Whitby and Scarborough at this date. In June 1933 the L&NER had converted ten old Great Northern Railway six-wheelers for use as camping coaches and two of them were sent to the Whitby-Loftus line where they could be parked at Cloughton, Stainton Dale, Robin Hood's Bay, Sandsend, Kettleness or Staines. The holidaymakers could move their coach between these stations during their holiday by requesting the Station Master to arrange this. The Second World War brought an immediate end to holidays in camping coaches and the business did not resume until 1952 when BR converted a number of former Great Eastern Railway eight-wheel non-corridor coaches, one of which was parked at Staithes. The gradient post by the lamp post between the signal box and No. 80117 shows that it has come up a 1 in 208 incline but will be faced with a climb of 1 in 59 when it leaves the station.

CHAPTER 8 - TO THE SEASIDE - WHITBY AND SCARBOROUGH

Sandsend

The Whitby to Middlesbrough line saw a variety of large tank engines during the 1950s with examples of LM&SR, British Railways and L&NER designs. One of the less common types was the Thompson 'L1' 2-6-4T. North British Locomotive Company built No. 67764 from February 1949 was at Middlesbrough for two years, from June 1956 until June 1958, and during this time was photographed after leaving Sandsend with a Whitby to Middlesbrough train. The station is in the centre background with two camping coaches visible and to the left of this is Sandsend viaduct and the seafront properties, which are still there today.

Cecil Ord/Rail Archive Stephenson

There were five steel tubular viaducts on the line, at Upgang, Newholm Bank, East Row and Sandsend; the latter was 268ft long, 63ft high and had eight spans. BR 4MT 2-6-4T No 80118 has just crossed the Sandsend viaduct with a Middlesbrough to Whitby train. It had been allocated to Whitby from new in June 1955 and was there until June 1958 when it moved to Neville Hill along with the other four of the class from Whitby, Nos. 80116-80117, 80119-80120. In the left background there are at least two camping coaches parked in Sandsend station and to their right is the entrance to the 1,652 yards' long Sandsend Tunnel.

Photo: *Cecil Ord/Rail Archive Stephenson*

The Esk Valley line

The inland route from Teesside to Whitby was completed in October 1865, running from Picton on the Northallerton to Stockton line to meet the line from Whitby-Pickering at Grosmont. This facilitated a regular passenger service between Whitby and Stockton/Middlesbrough which in 1950 amounted to five daily departures from Whitby, two of which ran through to Stockton via Picton and the other three reversed at Battersby to go up to Middlesbrough. In June 1954 the passenger service west of Battersby was withdrawn, forcing all trains to reverse at Battersby; the introduction of DMUs in May 1958 considerably simplified the operation of the service. In the first summer after closure of the coastal line between Loftus and Whitby there were around fifteen trains each way every day between Whitby and Middlesbrough which used the Esk Valley line.

'A8' 4-6-2T No. 69883 waits at Battersby during the period it was allocated to Stockton, between June 1950 and October 1952, after which it moved to Middlesbrough. The complex pointwork at the station, originally known as Ingleby Junction, then Battersby Junction from 1878 and finally plain Battersby in 1893, dated back to the provision of a large three-road engine shed (out of picture at the left) to serve the locomotives working iron ore traffic on the line. The shed was only operational until 1895 but the building itself was not demolished until 1965.

The driver of the Metropolitan-Cammell DMU in the bay platform at Battersby is carrying a number of token pouches in addition to his own token. The leading Motor Brake Second is No. E50166 which identifies the set as one of those built in January 1957 for use in the West Riding, but by early 1963 had been transferred to Darlington where it worked the Middlesbrough to Scarborough trains and the Guisborough Branch.

Castleton Moor

A Whitby-bound Metropolitan-Cammell DMU approaching Castleton Moor station on 6th May 1967.

Guisborough

A Metropolitan-Cammell DMU at Guisborough in around 1963. The station was opened in 1854 as the terminus of the Middlesbrough and Guisborough Railway and when the Cleveland Railway completed its line from the east at Loftus was left on a short spur from what now became a through route between Middlesbrough and Loftus. Trains calling at Guisborough had to reverse there and the introduction of DMUs in May 1958 simplified operation. Those from Middlesbrough ran into the straight into the station and then backed out to the junction before going forward again; in the other direction, they ran past the junction and then backed into the station so they could leave facing forwards. The Loftus to Guisborough passenger service was withdrawn in 1960 leaving Guisborough once again as the terminus at the end of the line from Middlesbrough. This service was withdrawn in March 1964 although freight traffic continued until August.

CHAPTER 8 - TO THE SEASIDE - WHITBY AND SCARBOROUGH

Whitby

The fishing port and resort of Whitby had two stations, Town and West Cliff, serving four different routes and connected in a quite distinctive way as the map and the pictures on this page show. The coast line north from West Cliff to Loftus closed in 1958, followed in March 1965 by the coastal line to Scarborough and the Malton-Grosmont route through Pickering, leaving only the Esk Valley line to Middlesbrough via Battersby.

An 'A8' 4-6-2T on the line from Grosmont with a fish van on the rear of the train. It is on the curve at the side of the River Esk approaching the 915ft long, 120ft high Larpool Viaduct. At the top right is the embankment carrying the line to Whitby West Cliff and Saltburn. Prospect Hill Junction was just beyond the bridge above the engine.

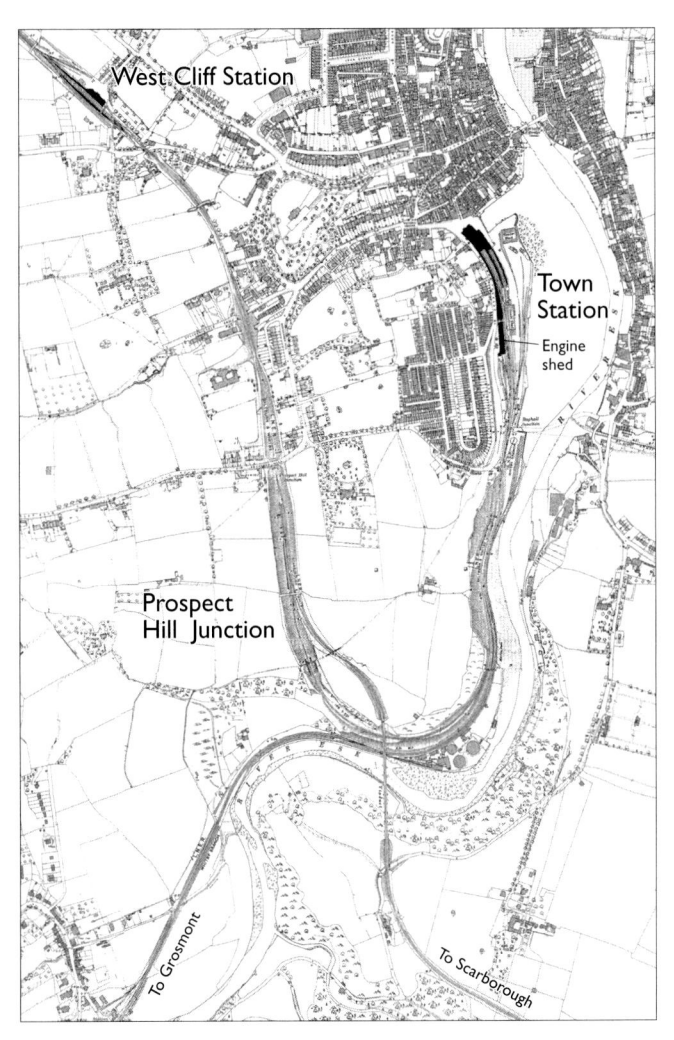

Larpool Viaduct from river level, with lines running through the second and fourth arches from left and over the top to Prospect Hill Junction from Scarborough; the gasworks is visible through the sixth arch.

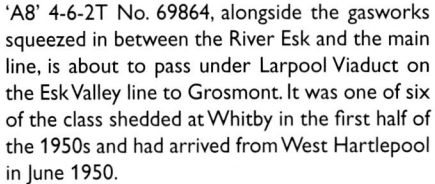

'A8' 4-6-2T No. 69864, alongside the gasworks squeezed in between the River Esk and the main line, is about to pass under Larpool Viaduct on the Esk Valley line to Grosmont. It was one of six of the class shedded at Whitby in the first half of the 1950s and had arrived from West Hartlepool in June 1950.

Two pictures taken on the same day in 1953 of trains approaching Prospect Hill Junction going towards West Cliff station having just crossed over Larpool Viaduct. 'J25' 0-6-0 No. 65647 which was built at Gateshead for the NER in 1898 has an easy task with just a single van and a brake van. This engine had an interesting history: it was withdrawn in April 1939 but re-instated when war broke out and loaned to the GWR as one of the replacements for the Dean Goods sent overseas. After it returned to the L&NER in 1946 it would remain in service for another decade and was at Whitby from June 1952 until October 1955.

'B1' 4-6-0 No. 61275 with a train from Scarborough. It entered service in the first month after nationalisation and was allocated to Stockton between November 1951 and November 1954.

Almost as soon as the line left Whitby Town station a single track up to West Cliff station diverged from the double track line to Grosmont and Pickering. It climbed steeply up to Prospect Hill Junction where it met the line from Scarborough which had crossed over Larpool Viaduct. BR Standard 2-6-4T No. 80118 takes a local from Whitby to Saltburn and Middlesbrough in the mid-1950s. It had been allocated to Whitby since it was delivered from Brighton in June 1955 and was there for three years before it was transferred to Leeds Neville Hill.

Whitby Abbey is just visible above the first coach of the train and the River Esk to the right as 'A8' 4-6-2T No. 69873 departs from the Town station in 1954, probably with a train to Middlesbrough. It was allocated there from November 1950 until July 1955 when it was transferred to West Hartlepool. No. 69873 had been rebuilt from 'H1' 4-4-4T No. 1520 in 1935 and it worked in this form until withdrawn in February 1960.

An immaculate 'A8' 4-6-2T No. 69861 at Whitby Town in April 1957. It was rebuilt from a 4-4-4T in 1935 and still has the original pattern of bunker with conventional coal rails. No. 69861 had been transferred from Whitby to Malton in June 1956 and was working home with a coaching set branded 'Malton-Whitby'.

One of Whitby shed's five BR Standard 2-6-4Ts No. 80117 backing its train out at the end of the day to the carriage sidings in April 1957.

CHAPTER 8 - TO THE SEASIDE - WHITBY AND SCARBOROUGH

The driver and fireman of 'B1' 4-6-0 No. 61021 *Reitbok* enjoy the summer sunshine as they wait for departure time in Platform 2 at Whitby Town in 1964. No. 61021 had been allocated to York since September 1960 and was withdrawn from there in June 1967. On the right, a holiday maker and his son make their way to the front of the Metropolitan-Cammell DMU.

Whitby shed

The shed, coded 50G under British Railways, was opened in 1868. It closed in April 1959 when DMUs took over the Pickering/Malton service and was then used as a fish packing warehouse. The allocation in 1949 was five 'G5' 0-4-4Ts and six 'A8' 4-6-2Ts, five of which had been transferred there in mid-1948. Five 'J25' 0-6-0s arrived between 1951 and 1953, but the biggest change came in 1954/55 when several BR Standards arrived, five brand new 2-6-4Ts and four Class '3' 2-6-0s, although one of the latter was there only for a month or so and was replaced by another. The three Fairburn 2-6-4Ts working in the Darlington to Middlesbrough area also spent time on the shed's books between late 1955 and 1959.

Still with its L&NER shed allocation on the buffer beam and no British Railways' cast shedplate, 'A8' 4-6-2T No. 69888 in front of Whitby shed in April 1949, almost a year after it had been transferred there from Middlesbrough. Built in 1921 as a 4-4-4T and rebuilt in 1934 as an 'A8', it was newly outshopped from Darlington after a General overhaul during which it was fitted with a 63A boiler and renumbered as No. 69888.

Whitby to Scarborough

The Scarborough & Whitby Railway opened the line via Ravenscar and Robin Hood's Bay in 1885, many years after it was first mooted in 1848. The line, with gradients as steep as 1 in 39, was difficult to work in bad weather and was particularly susceptible to mist and sea fog. Even with short two-coach trains there were many instances of trains stalling, especially in the tunnels.

Climbing to Ravenscar

'B1' 4-6-0 No 61173 climbs the 1 in 41 of Ravenscar Bank with a Whitby to Scarborough train in September 1954. It was one of the class built at Vulcan Foundry and entered service in June 1947. At this date No. 61173 was allocated to Stockton and remained there until June 1959 when it went to Thornaby.
T.G. Hepburn/Rail Archive Stephenson

NER class 'A8' 4-6-2T No. 69867 climbs Ravenscar Bank with a Whitby to Scarborough train in September 1954. It was built at Darlington in 1914 as an 'H1' 4-4-4T No. 2160 and was rebuilt to a 4-6-2T in 1936. No. 69867 was allocated to Scarborough between July 1951 and withdrawal at the end of 1959, except for two short spells away at Selby in 1951 and Hull Botanic Gardens in 1955.
T.G. Hepburn/Rail Archive Stephenson

BR Standard Class '3' 2-6-0 No. 77012 climbs up to Ravenscar with a Darlington to Scarborough express on 2nd September 1954, less than three months after it entered traffic allocated to Darlington. When first introduced, the class was regularly used on the Darlington to Saltburn and Scarborough services, and monopolised the 8.0am from Darlington, returning with the 7.1pm from Scarborough. However, this did not last for long and seven of them were transferred to West Auckland in July/August to work over the Stainmore line to Tebay. No. 77012 was the last to leave Darlington, moving to West Auckland in January 1955.
T.G. Hepburn/Rail Archive Stephenson

Ravenscar

Ivatt '4MT' 2-6-0 No. 43072 waits at Ravenscar with a southbound service in the mid-1950s. Schoolgirls carrying suitcases have left the train on their way to Fyling Hall School, a co-educational boarding school near Robin Hood's Bay. There was a station at Fyling Hall but this became an unstaffed halt in 1958 and presumably it was easier for them to use Ravenscar. No. 43072 was built at Darlington in September 1950; it was at Middlesbrough from March 1951 until June 1958.

Hayburn Wyke

BR Standard '4MT' 2-6-4T No. 80117 pulls away from Hayburn Wyke with a Whitby to Scarborough train on 2nd September 1954. In March 1953 Hayburn Wyke became an unstaffed Halt and the station building was converted to holiday accommodation after electricity was installed for the first time. The hotel in the right background is still open today, trading as the 'Hayburn Wyke Inn'. *T.G. Hepburn/Rail Archive Stephenson*

Cloughton

'B1' 4-6-0 No. 61256 arriving at Cloughton from Scarborough with an inspection saloon on 10th September 1964. No. 61256 had been transferred to York from Hull Dairycoates a few days before this picture was taken. Cloughton station building, goods shed and the stationmaster's house have all been renovated since closure in 1965. The house and goods shed are now a luxurious Bed & Breakfast hotel and there is even a BR Mark 1 coach parked there as a '4-star luxury camping coach' named '*Oscar*' providing self-catering accommodation.

Seamer

Trains to Scarborough from the south and east reached the town via Seamer which was about three miles inland. The line from York via Malton had opened in 1845 followed a year later by a line from Seamer to Filey. By 1847 after the line from Filey to Bridlington was opened, trains could run from Scarborough to Hull. The third line to reach Seamer was the Forge Valley line from Pickering which met the Bridlington line at Seamer Junction. This was first mooted in 1864 by the Scarborough & Whitby Railway but nothing happened for many years and it was eventually built by the North Eastern Railway, opening in 1882; the line, which served only lightly populated villages with stations well away from the villages themselves, was closed in 1950.

The Gresley 'D49' 4-4-0s were regular motive power on the trains between Scarborough and Hull. No. 62720 *Cambridgeshire*, approaching Seamer station in around 1954, was allocated to Botanic Gardens shed throughout the 1950s, moving to Dairycoates in June 1959. It was built in 1928 as a 'D49/3' with Lentz Oscillating Cam poppet valves but was rebuilt to a 'D49/1' in the late-1930s with Walschaerts' valve gear and Gresley's derived motion. Fish vans like the two at the front of this train were often conveyed on passenger services in this area.

'B16/3' 4-6-0 No. 61464 approaching Seamer station from Scarborough in the mid-1950s with a mixed rake of mainly L&NER stock. No. 61464 was built by the L&NER in December 1923 and had been at York since 1943 and only left there in 1961. The 'B16/3' was a Thompson modification to the Raven North Eastern Railway 'B16' design with individual sets of outside Walschaerts valve gear for each cylinder in place of the original Stephenson inside motion.

'D49/2' 4-4-0 No. 62739 *The Badsworth* leaves a trail of thick black smoke over Musham Bank Cottages near the line just to the north of Seamer station. It was one of the final forty engines of the 'D49' class that were fitted with Lentz Rotary Cam poppet valves. No. 62739 was shedded at Scarborough from July 1951 until withdrawn in October 1960.

This picture was taken from the road overbridge which is just visible in the left background through the smoke in the picture above. Hull Botanic Gardens' 'B1' 4-6-0 No. 61305 is heading towards Scarborough in around 1957.

CHAPTER 8 - TO THE SEASIDE - WHITBY AND SCARBOROUGH

A Brush Type '4' approaches Seamer from the Scarborough direction in around 1966. As it is displaying reporting number 1S48 it is almost certainly a Summer Saturdays Only Scarborough to Glasgow Queen Street train.

BR Sulzer Type '2' No. D5176 at Seamer with a trip freight, probably on the same date as the picture above. This was the first of what became the Class '25' to be built with an engine rated at 1,250bhp, up from 1,160bhp in the earlier locomotives, and new smaller, lighter AEI 253AY traction motors. Although the body shell remained similar to Nos. D5151-D5175, there were a number of minor changes: the air horns were moved to either side of the headcode panel, the cab skirt and body fairing were discontinued, and the fuel and water tanks were re-designed. No. D5176 entered service from Darlington Works in January 1963 allocated to Holbeck. This photograph was probably taken while it was at York between June 1963 and December 1966. There are four steel-carrying trestle wagons, one a bogie well, in the train carrying traffic for Wards of Sherburn. The wagons were shunted out at Weaverthorpe sidings which remained open until 1981, the station having closed over fifty years earlier.

Scarborough

The first station in Scarborough opened in 1845 at the end of the line from York built by George Hudson's York & North Midland Railway; a year later after the line from Filey to Bridlington was opened, through trains began to run between Scarborough and Hull. The Whitby & Scarborough Railway opened in 1885 to provide a link to the north. The station was continuously extended between 1859 and 1902, by which date it had increased to nine platforms. It was renamed as Scarborough Central in 1926.

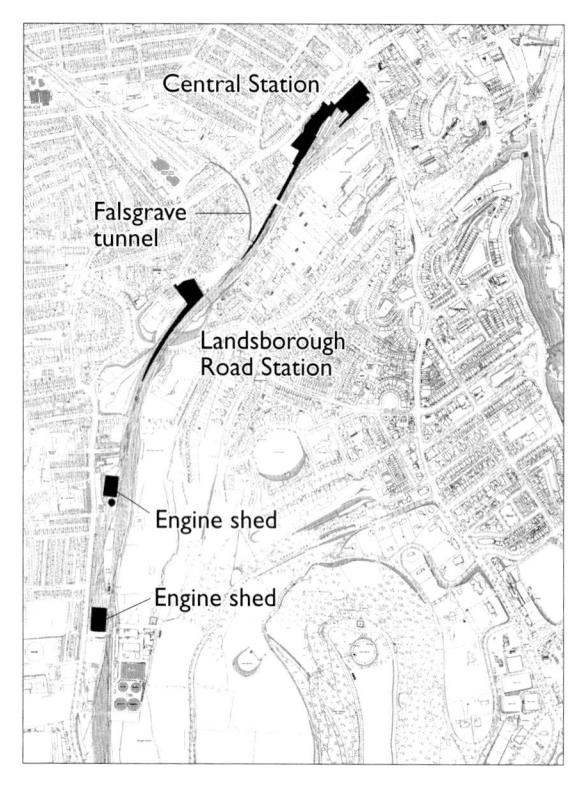

'B1' 4-6-0 No. 61069 from York shed approaching Scarborough with the 8.30am SO from Manchester Victoria to the excursion station at Scarborough Londesborough Road on 17th April 1962.

Scarborough was host to holiday traffic from the industrial centres of the East Midlands and South Yorkshire. Arriving with a train full of holidaymakers in the mid-1950s Hughes-Fowler 'Crab' 2-6-0 No. 42902 runs under the second of the impressive signal gantries on the approach to Central station; it will then pass the engine shed which is off camera to the right. The train consists mainly of ex-L&NER stock apart from a BR Mark 1 Third. No. 42902 was at Rowsley from 1942 until 1959, except for a few odd weeks at Kettering in mid-1954.

CHAPTER 8 - TO THE SEASIDE - WHITBY AND SCARBOROUGH

Immingham 'B1' 4-6-0 No. 61089 approaching Scarborough, passing Gasworks signal box with the gasworks on the left, probably in 1965. Note that the signals on the North Eastern Railway-built gantry, the first one on the approach, have been de-commissioned and lost their arms. The signal box was closed in March 1965.

'D49/1' 4-4-0 No. 62703 *Hertfordshire* has just passed Falsgrave signal box as it arrives at Scarborough in the mid-1950s. It was allocated to Bridlington from November 1950 until October 1957.
T.G. Hepburn/Rail Archive Stephenson

Perched on the wall with a superb view of the activity below, a young spotter watches the arrival of 'B16/1' 4-6-0 No. 61423 with a train from Leeds in the mid-1950s. It was allocated to York from the 1940s right up to withdrawal in September 1961. The sign above the two older spotters on the right reads 'To Platform 1A – Train for intermediate stations to Whitby (West Cliff) and Middlesbrough'. The long platform was cut out of Platform 1 in May 1934 to allow trains from Whitby access to the station without crossing the main approach tracks; before this they used the short bay platforms, Nos 7, 8 or 9.
Kenneth Field/ Rail Archive Stephenson

Falsgrave Tunnel and Whitby trains

When the Scarborough & Whitby Railway built its line between the two towns, it did not build its own stations at each end and instead used those owned by the North Eastern Railway which caused operating difficulties which lasted until the end of steam working. At Scarborough, the station was accessed through the Falsgrave Tunnel. On departures to Whitby the engine, after drawing out of the station, had to run round its train opposite Londesborough Road station to gain access to the junction for the Whitby line. In 1934 a special platform, numbered 1A, was built which enabled engines to propel their trains into and out of the station without needing to run round and cross the main approach lines.

The Falsgrave signalman waits to exchange the token as 'A8' 4-6-2T No. 69881 comes out of Falsgrave Tunnel with a Whitby to Scarborough train. The locomotive will draw the train forward, then push it back into Scarborough Central Platform 1A. The tunnel was around 260 yards long and curved round to Gallows Close goods yard.
Kenneth Field/Rail Archive Stephenson

CHAPTER 8 - TO THE SEASIDE - WHITBY AND SCARBOROUGH

Father and son railway enthusiasts chat to the driver of 'A8' 4-6-2T No. 69867 which has just reversed into the long Falsgrave Platform 1A with a train from Whitby as classmate No. 69885 performs station pilot duties in around 1957. Both engines were allocated to Scarborough for most of the 1950s, except for two short spells away. No. 69867 was there from July 1951 until withdrawn at the end of 1959 and No. 69885 from June 1952 until withdrawal in June 1960. There was a quarter mile long walk to reach the end of Platform 1A from the booking office and this was reflected in the timetable with the departure times in the working timetable three minutes later than those shown in the public version.

T.G. Hepburn/Rail Archive Stephenson

Lenz Rotary Cam poppet valve gear 'D49/2' 4-4-0 No. 62751 *The Albrighton* storms out of Scarborough Central past the Falsgrave signal box and under the NER signal gantry, both made listed structures in 1986. No. 62751 was built at Darlington in July 1934 and was allocated to Scarborough from June 1949 until withdrawn in March 1959. The signal box, which assumed control of the station approach lines at the gantry, was a North Eastern Railway Type 4 with 120 levers built in 1908 and in operation until 2010. It was restored in 2007 at a cost of £180,000 and repainted in North Eastern Region Oriental Blue and cream. The entrance to Falsgrave tunnel is to the left of the box. The gantry has also been saved and after it was taken out of use in 2010 was moved to Grosmont on the North Yorkshire Moors Railway where it has been restored to operational use, albeit with a shorter span than when it was at Falsgrave.

CHAPTER 8 - TO THE SEASIDE - WHITBY AND SCARBOROUGH

Backing down from the shed after turning and refuelling, BR Standard Class '5' 4-6-0 No. 73054 on 21st June 1954. It had only entered service that month and was allocated to Holbeck where it stayed until August 1955, transferring to Derby.

Two spotters in one of the favourite locations at the end of Platform 1A next to BR Standard Class '3' 2-6-0 No. 77010 on 11th July 1954. This was only a month after it entered traffic allocated to Darlington along with seven of its classmates. They quickly settled down to work on the Darlington to Saltburn and Scarborough services, but their stay was brief and seven of them including No. 77010 were transferred to West Auckland in July/August to work over the Stainmore line to Tebay.

'D49/1' 4-4-0 No. 62707 *Lancashire* arriving at Scarborough in the late 1950s. when it was allocated to Hull Botanic Gardens. This view shows that the railway and station were situated high above the town.

On station pilot duties, BR Standard Class '3' 2-6-2T No. 82028 had been transferred from Darlington to Scarborough along with No. 82026 in September 1958 after being displaced by DMUs. One was used as Gallows Close goods pilot in the morning and on the 2.45 pm to Hull in the afternoon, whilst the other was often used as the station pilot. They were joined by Nos. 82027 and 82029 from Malton in June 1960. Nos. 82028 and 82029 were transferred to Malton in September 1961 and did not return.

CHAPTER 8 - TO THE SEASIDE - WHITBY AND SCARBOROUGH

'B16/1' 4-6-0 No. 61428 at Scarborough Central in April 1957. It was at Leeds Neville Hill from August 1949 until withdrawal in October 1960. No. 61428 is in Platform 3 with the shorter Platforms 4 to 9 only partly visible behind the signal box; the small goods yard is on the extreme right. Platforms 6 to 9 were added in 1902 when the goods depot which formerly occupied the site was closed after the Gallows Close goods depot was opened. Scarborough signal box controlled only the immediate station area and access to the goods yard with the Falsgrave box taking over for the approach lines out to Gasworks signal box. In the background is the 1884 clock tower of the Grade II listed station and to the right, the imposing five-storey high Pavilion Hotel, for many years one of the resort's most luxurious hotels, which was demolished in 1973.

Whitby's BR Standard 2-6-4T No. 80117 alongside York's 'B16/2' 4-6-0 No. 61437 in early 1958 before the 2-6-4T moved away to Leeds Neville Hill in June. No. 61437 was one of the Gresley rebuilds of the Raven 'B16', replacing the Stephenson valve gear with Walschaerts gear and derived motion for the inside cylinder. Note the difference in platform height on either side of No. 80117; Platform 1 is on the left and Platform 2 on the right.

A view towards the platforms of Scarborough Central as York 'B1' No. 61069 departs in 1963. Diesels are much in evidence in the background, a Sulzer Type '2' nearest the camera, a 204bhp shunter and two DMUs in the platforms. No. 61069 was allocated to York for its last four years in traffic and was withdrawn in August 1963.

A Metropolitan-Cammell DMU arrives in Platform 6 on 22nd August 1964. The longer Platforms on the right, Nos 1 and 2, were added in 1883 to accommodate the growing excursion traffic. The roof over them was demolished in January 1971 after it was severely damaged by gale force winds during the previous month.

This picture of English Electric Type '4' No. D286 in Platform 2 was probably taken while it was allocated to York between March and October 1967. It spent most of its time either at York or Gateshead and was withdrawn in March 1984 as No. 40086. Behind the train and the extended roof over the two long platforms can be glimpsed the large circulating area then used for road vehicles, with a number of vans and lorries parked there.

English Electric Type '3' No. D6808 waits in Platform 2 in around 1968. It was allocated to Tinsley from new in January 1963 and was there until 1978 when it left for Scotland. It was renumbered three times, to No. 37108 in 1974, No. 37325 when it was fitted with re-geared cast frame CP7 bogies in 1986 and then back to No. 37108 in 1989. It survived into preservation and was recently restored to working order at Crewe Heritage Centre. Immediately above No. D6808, the longest station seat in Great Britain can just be discerned; it extended to no less than 456 feet!

It seems unlikely that the large crowd on Platform 1A has been attracted by the 'O3' shunter and its dropside wagon runner. It is out-stationed from York TMD but will have to return for re-fuelling, probably just once a fortnight during the summer. Its use was primarily to release train engines from incoming excursions, but it would also shunt the remaining yards.

Scarborough shed and carriage sidings

'Jubilee' 4-6-0 No. 45605 *Cyprus* had brought in a train from the East Midlands on 1st August 1954. It was built with a Stanier 4,000 gallon tender which was exchanged with a Fowler 3,500 gallon tender from 'Royal Scot' No. 6113 in June 1937. The eight-road shed, which housed twenty-four engines, was opened in 1890 to supplement the earlier roundhouse. Although the shed closed in May 1963, the yard continued to be used as a servicing point for visiting steam locomotives until 1966 when the buildings were demolished.

Summer Saturdays up to the late 1950s saw engines which were normally only used for freight work pressed into use to take holidaymakers to the coast. No. 44245, a LM&SR '4F' 0-6-0 from Canklow shed rests on shed before taking its train back to Sheffield in 1954 or 1955. It had been transferred from Hellifield to Canklow in April 1954 and stayed there until withdrawn in May 1962.

Three of Scarborough shed's big 'A8' 4-6-2Ts, Nos. 69867, 69877 and 69885, near the end of their days in the roundhouse on 13th June 1959 and they would probably do little – if any – further work before they were all withdrawn at the end of the year. The roundhouse shed was opened in 1881 and the bigger straight road shed added in 1890; it was coded 50E after nationalisation.

'B1' 4-6-0 No. 61020 *Gemsbok* from York shed doesn't disturb the permanent way men as it backs in to the station past Falsgrave signal box in the 1950s. Three youngsters have a good view as they dangle over the wall in front of the CAWG sign on the hostel for the Christian Alliance of Women and Girls. No. 61020 was named after the Gemsbok, also known as an Oryx Gazelle, a large antelope of striking appearance with long, spearlike horns and native to the arid areas and deserts of Southern Africa. The L&NER clearly got confused with these native names as No. 61004 was named *Oryx* and was effectively the same animal!

CHAPTER 8 - TO THE SEASIDE - WHITBY AND SCARBOROUGH

'D49/1' 4-4-0 No. 62735 *Westmorland* leaving Scarborough on 29th August 1953 passes Londesborough Road station, out of picture on the left. The station was opened in 1908 to cope with the increasing volume of holiday traffic which the main Central station could not handle and was in use until August 1963. Some of the coaches behind No. 62735 are still in L&NER teak with pre-nationalisation insignia and therefore are likely to be excursion stock brought into use for a few weeks during the summer.

The young signalman in Gasworks signal box waves to the fireman of Thompson 'B1' 4-6-0 No. 61037 *Jairou* as it takes another load of holidaymakers home from Scarborough. In the background is the gantry in the earlier picture of No. 42902, at the south end of the shed. Gasworks signal box closed in March 1965.

A 'B16' in original condition with Stephenson valve gear, No. 61427 heads away from Scarborough with the carriage sidings in the distance on the left. There are two short-wheelbase vans carrying fish and a full brake at the head of the train in the mid-1950s. No. 61427 was allocated to Leeds Neville Hill from August 1949 up to withdrawal in March 1960.

LM&SR Class '5' 4-6-0 No. 45333 is captured by two cameras as it gets into its stride after passing the carriage sidings. The picture was taken during the six months it was allocated to Nottingham shed, between June and December 1959. No. 45333 was built by Armstrong, Whitworth in March 1937, one of 227 engines in the largest single order placed by a British railway company.